ᴛʜᴇ**new** biology

Animal Cloning

Revised Edition

THE new biology

Animal Cloning

The Science of Nuclear Transfer
Revised Edition

JOSEPH PANNO, PH.D.

Facts On File
An imprint of Infobase Publishing

ANIMAL CLONING: The Science of Nuclear Transfer, Revised Edition

Facts On File, Inc.
An imprint of Infobase Publishing
132 West 31st Street
New York NY 10001

Library of Congress Cataloging-in-Publication Data
Panno, Joseph
    Animal cloning : the science of nuclear transfer / Joseph Panno.—Rev. ed.
        p. cm.—(The new biology)
    Includes bibliographical references and index.
    ISBN 978-0-8160-6847-0 (alk. paper)
    1. Cloning—Popular works. 2. Cell nuclei—Transplantation—Popular works. I. Title.
    QH442.2.P26 2011
    660.6'5—dc22   2009049945

Facts On File books are available at special discounts when purchased in bulk quantities for businesses, associations, institutions, or sales promotions. Please call our Special Sales Department in New York at (212) 967-8800 or (800) 322-8755.

You can find Facts On File on the World Wide Web at http://www.factsonfile.com

Excerpts included herewith have been reprinted by permission of the copyright holders; the author has made every effort to contact copyright holders. The publishers will be glad to rectify, in future editions, any errors or omissions brought to their notice.

Text design by Erik Lindstrom
Composition by Hermitage Publishing Services
Illustrations by the author
Photo research by Diane K. French
Cover printed by Bang Printing, Brainerd, Minn.
Book printed and bound by Bang Printing, Brainerd, Minn.
Date printed: October 2010
Printed in the United States of America

10 9 8 7 6 5 4 3 2 1

Contents

Preface

When the first edition of this set was being written, the new biology was just beginning to come into its potential and to experience some of its first failures. Dolly the sheep was alive and well and had just celebrated her fifth birthday. Stem cell researchers, working 12-hour days, were giddy with the prospect of curing every disease known to humankind, but were frustrated by inconsistent results and the limited availability of human embryonic stem cells. Gene therapists, still reeling from the disastrous Gelsinger trial of 1998, were busy trying to figure out what had gone wrong and how to improve the safety of a procedure that many believed would revolutionize medical science. And cancer researchers, while experiencing many successes, hit their own speed bump when a major survey showed only modest improvements in the prognosis for all of the deadliest cancers.

During the 1970s, when the new biology was born, recombinant technology served to reenergize the sagging discipline that biology had become. This same level of excitement reappeared in the 1990s with the emergence of gene therapy, the cloning of Dolly the sheep, and the successful cultivation of stem cells. Recently, great excitement has come with the completion of the human genome project and the genome sequencing of more than 100 animal and plant species. Careful analysis of these genomes has spawned a new branch of biological research known as comparative genomics. The information that scientists can now extract from animal genomes is expected to improve all other branches of biological science. Not to be outdone, stem cell researchers have found a way to produce embryo-like stem cells from ordinary skin cells. This achievement not only marks the end of the great stem cell debate, but it also provides an immensely powerful procedure, known as cellular dedifferentiation, for studying and manipulating the very essence of a cell. This procedure will become a crucial weapon in the fight against cancer and many other diseases.

The new biology, like our expanding universe, has been growing and spreading at an astonishing rate. The amount of information that is now available on these topics is of astronomical proportions. Thus, the problem of deciding what to leave out has become as difficult as the decision of what to include. The guiding principle in writing this set has always been to provide a thorough overview of the topics without overwhelming the reader with a mountain of facts and figures. To be sure, this set contains many facts and figures, but these have been carefully chosen to illustrate only the essential principles.

This edition, in keeping with the expansion of the biological disciplines, has grown to accommodate new material and new areas of research. Four new books have been added that focus on areas of biological research that are reaping the benefits of genome science and modern research technologies. Thus, the New Biology set now consists of the following 10 volumes:

Many new chapters have been added to each of the original six volumes, and the remaining chapters have been extensively revised and updated. The number of figures and photos in each book has increased significantly, and all are now rendered in full color. The new volumes, following the same format as the originals, greatly expand the scope of the New Biology set and serve to emphasize the fact that these technologies are not just about finding cures for diseases but are helping scientists understand a wide range of biological processes. Even a partial list of these revelations is impressive: detailed information on every gene and every protein that is needed to build a human being; eventual identification of all cancer genes, stem cell–specific genes, and longevity genes; mapping of safe chromosomal insertion sites for gene therapy; and the identification of genes that control the growth of the human brain, the development of speech, and the maintenance of mental stability. In a stunning achievement, genome researchers have been able to trace the exact route our human ancestors used to emigrate from Africa nearly 65,000 years ago and even to estimate the number of individuals who made up the original group.

In addition to the accelerating pace of discovery, the new biology has made great strides in resolving past mistakes and failures. The Gelsinger trial was a dismal failure that killed a young man in the prime of his life, but gene therapy trials in the next 10 years will be astonishing, both for their success and for their safety. For the past 50 years, cancer researchers have been caught in a desperate struggle as they tried to control the growth and spread of deadly tumors, but many scientists are now confident that cancer will be eliminated by 2020. Viruses, such as HIV or the flu, are resourceful and often deadly adversaries, but genome researchers are about to put the fight on more rational grounds as detailed information is obtained about viral genes, viral life cycles, and viruses' uncanny ability to evade or cripple the human immune system.

These struggles and more are covered in this edition of the New Biology set. I hope the discourse will serve to illustrate both the power of science and the near superhuman effort that has gone into the creation and validation of these technologies.

Acknowledgments

I would first like to thank the legions of science graduate students and postdoctoral fellows who have made the new biology a practical reality. They are the unsung heroes of this discipline. The clarity and accuracy of the initial manuscript for this book was much improved by reviews and comments from Diana Dowsley, Michael Panno, Rebecca Lapres, and later by Frank K. Darmstadt, executive editor, and the rest of the Facts On File staff. I am also indebted to Diane K. French and Elizabeth Oakes for their help in securing photographs for the New Biology set. Finally, as always, I would like to thank my wife and daughter for keeping the ship on an even keel.

Introduction

Nature has been cloning animals, cells, and molecules for millions of years. Scientists got into the act just 34 years ago, when John Gurdon, a professor at Cambridge University in England, cloned a frog. Gurdon's experiment did not generate a great deal of interest at the time and was rarely discussed outside the world of research labs. In 1996, when Ian Wilmut, a British biologist working at the Roslin Institute in Scotland, cloned a sheep named Dolly, the reaction was dramatically different. The news of Dolly's birth was reported in every major newspaper and magazine around the world, and she quickly became the most celebrated (and certainly the most photographed) lamb in the history of animal husbandry. Wilmut was invited to speak before the Parliament of the United Kingdom and the Congress of the United States, after which, the team leaders were interviewed to the point of exhaustion. Cloning a mammal sparked the public's imagination in a way that had not been seen since American astronauts got their white suits dirty on the surface of the moon. Cloning a sheep, unlike cloning a frog, brought the technology closer to home, making it both fascinating and frightening to a great many people.

The ability to clone a mammal was the culmination of research in cell and developmental biology that stretched back to the late 1800s. The idea of cloning an animal was originated by the German embryologist Hans Spemann in 1898 as a way of testing the developmental capacity of an adult cell nucleus and whether such a nucleus lost genes during the process of embryonic development. The techniques available in Spemann's time were not adequate to fully explore this question. Moreover, very little was known about the cell and, in particular, about the process of cell division. This information came only after the introduction of recombinant DNA technology in the 1970s. By the 1990s enough had been learned about the cell and the properties of cell division to make mammalian cloning a possibility.

Although Gurdon cloned a frog as a way to study embryonic development, interest in cloning technology today is quite different and is focused on four applications. The first involves the cloning of farm animals in such a way that foreign genes are introduced into their cells so they can produce therapeutically useful proteins, such as blood clotting factors to treat hemophilia. Wilmut's team has already cloned animals for this purpose. The second application involves the cloning of livestock to produce a herd of cattle or dairy cows that possess desirable traits. The third application involves a procedure known as therapeutic cloning, whereby human embryos are produced for the purpose of harvesting stem cells, a special kind of cell that may be used to treat many diseases. The fourth application, known as reproductive cloning, involves cloning humans to replace loved ones or to re-create especially talented individuals.

The first two applications of cloning technology are already in progress, but the last two have become extremely controversial and are currently the subject of extensive debate by the general public, as well as by legislators, philosophers, and ethicists. Several countries, the United States and the United Kingdom included, have either passed laws to ban reproductive and therapeutic cloning or they are in the process of debating the advisability of such laws. The consensus view would have reproduction cloning banned, but such legislation has been difficult to pass, particularly in the United States, where many fear that it will automatically restrict or ban therapeutic cloning.

Human cloning, like human abortion, will be discussed, debated, and argued over for a very long time, and this is as it should be. The issues are complex and extremely important, and although laws may be passed to regulate the technology, society as a whole may never find the legal solutions satisfactory. This is not surprising given some of the questions and speculations that arise when we consider cloning human beings: How many human embryos would a scientist have to sacrifice in order to produce one successful clone? Where are the human embryos for human cloning experiments going to come from, and who will decide how they are to be used? Are cloned farm animals normal, or are they prone to early aging and disease? If they are not normal, should we expect the same for human clones? If a human adult were cloned, would the child be born with its clone-parent's memories, and are they in fact the same person? Does a clone-child have the same legal rights as a natural-born child?

Animal Cloning, Revised Edition, one volume in the New Biology set, discusses all aspects of animal cloning, including the scientific, ethical, and legal issues. This edition contains updated and revised material throughout. Many new figures and photos have been added, and all are now in color. Beginning chapters discuss cloning within the context of a natural process that many animals use as a survival strategy, followed by the historical development of the nuclear transfer procedure, the cloning of Dolly the sheep, the medical applications of cloning technology and, finally, the ethical and legal debate.

Chapter 1 is renamed "A World Full of Clones" in order to emphasize the pervasiveness of natural clones in the world. In addition, a new section on plant clones has been added to this chapter. Two new chapters (6 and 9) have been added: Chapter 6 discusses therapeutic cloning and the recent production of the very controversial human-animal hybrids that scientists hope will make therapeutic cloning a practical reality. Chapter 9 profiles four companies that are involved in animal cloning and the production of transgenic drugs. Not all cloning enterprises are successful, and this chapter discusses some of the problems involved in trying to bring transgenic products to market. As before, the final chapter provides background material on cell biology, biotechnology, and other topics that are relevant to animal cloning. The cell biology and biotechnology primers have been extensively revised and condensed to improve the clarity of this important background information.

In 2004, when the first edition of this book was published, most scientists in the field were convinced that therapeutic cloning would lead to medical therapies by 2010, but this has not happened, nor is it likely to in the near or distant future. Much of the optimism was fueled by dramatic results reported by scientists in South Korea but which turned out to be fraudulent. In addition, scientists in Japan have discovered a way to reprogram skin cells into something equivalent to embryonic stem cells, which could make therapeutic cloning obsolete. On the other hand, several companies, profiled in chapter 9, have made real progress in their quest to produce badly needed drugs from cloned transgenic animals.

1

A World Full of Clones

The term *clone* is a well-known, emotionally charged word that has an aura of mystery and sinister intent. A clone sounds like something from another world—superhuman, frightening, and not quite lovable. This impression is no doubt related to the fact that clones are a favorite topic of science fiction films, the most famous being the robotic clone armies of *I, Robot* (2004), the *Star Wars* film series (Episode II, 2002), as well as the human clones in *Blade Runner* (1982) and *The Boys from Brazil* (1978). *Blade Runner* is an ominous futuristic tale about a group of human android clones, stationed off-world, who return to Earth to confront, and eventually, to kill their creator. *The Boys from Brazil* is a dark and sinister tale about an ex-Nazi doctor who clones several copies of Adolf Hitler with obvious evil intent.

Despite these fantastical stories, clones are all around, yet none of them have tried to destroy humankind or to re-create evil tyrants. Identical twins are clones, and most cells, whether living as individuals or as a part of a larger organism, reproduce by cloning themselves. This has always been the case with prokaryotes and is true of many eukaryotes as well. Moreover, cells replace their proteins by decoding the information that is stored in their genes. Each time a particular protein is produced, it is identical to previous copies and is, in effect, a clone. The production of proteins in this way is one of nature's most successful cloning experiments.

Scientists can now produce animal clones, but they began by making DNA clones, which form the very heart of biotechnology and paved the way for the birth of Dolly. To understand the full consequences of cloning technology, it is necessary to understand how it came to be that nature and scientists have produced such a wide range of clones, from tiny molecules to half-ton dairy cows.

MOLECULAR CLONES

Three of the most important molecular clones are proteins, DNA (deoxyribonucleic acid), and RNA (ribonucleic acid). Proteins are macromolecules, or very large molecules, that are used to build and run the cell. DNA is a macromolecule that is found in all cells, where it is used to encode an organism's genes. Each gene encodes the information for the production of a single protein. RNA is a macromolecule that is closely related to DNA and plays an important role in protein synthesis. As for proteins, each RNA is encoded by a single gene. Cells produce a great variety of molecular clones as evidenced by the number of genes they possess, which varies from a few thousand in bacteria to more than 30,000 in humans. Decoding a gene requires two steps, known as transcription and translation. Transcription is a process whereby the gene is copied into messenger RNA (mRNA), which is translated into a specific protein by ribosomes, special biomachines located in the cytoplasm of every cell.

The organization of protein synthesis is analogous to the organization of a carpentry shop, whereby a carpenter makes a photocopy of a blueprint for a table or a chair. The carpenter then takes

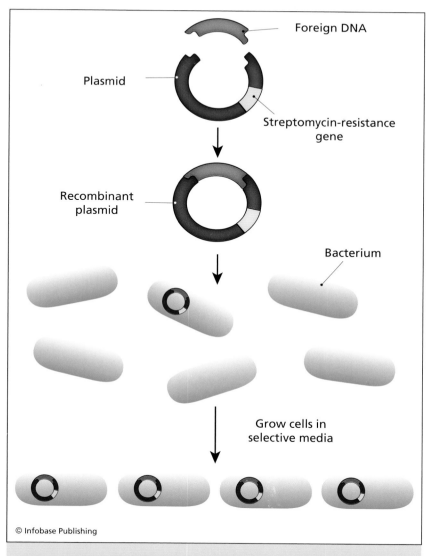

Foreign DNA

Plasmid

Streptomycin-resistance gene

Recombinant plasmid

Bacterium

Grow cells in selective media

© Infobase Publishing

Cloning DNA in a plasmid. The foreign DNA and the plasmid are cut with the same restriction enzyme, allowed to fuse, and then sealed with DNA ligase. The recombinant plasmid is mixed with bacterial cells, some of which pick up the plasmid, allowing them to grow in a culture medium containing streptomycin. For clarity, the bacteria's main chromosome is not shown, and the size of the plasmid, relative to the cell, is exaggerated.

the photocopy out to the shop floor, where it is used to construct the item of interest without jeopardizing the safety of the original blueprint. The proteins and RNA that run and build a cell have short lives, but when they wear out, exact duplicates can always be made. A third process called replication duplicates the DNA each time the cell divides. Thus translation and replication are two mechanisms by which the cell clones its own molecules.

Scientists produce DNA clones through the application of recombinant DNA technology. This technology provides a way to isolate a specific DNA sequence, which is then inserted into mini-chromosomes, called plasmids. The bacterium *Escherichia coli* is then coaxed into taking up these plasmids and amplifying them many millions of times. The amplified, or cloned, DNA sequence can then be isolated from the bacteria for further study. The amplified sequence is an exact clone of the original because the bacterium replicates the plasmid, along with the inserted piece of DNA, just as though it were part of its own chromosome. Scientists began cloning DNA in the 1970s, and though it may seem unlikely, the amplification of DNA in the laboratory has revolutionized biology and many other disciplines.

CELL CLONES

Any cell that reproduces asexually is a clone. Bacteria reproduce by binary fission, which is an asexual mode of reproduction. Consequently, bacteria, and indeed all prokaryotes, represent the largest group of clonal organisms on Earth. The fact that bacteria reproduce by cloning themselves seems to be at odds with their amazing adaptability and, in the case of pathogenic bacteria, their ability to develop resistance to antibiotics. A strain of *Staphylococcus aureus* has been isolated from a hospital ward, which is resistant to all known clinical antibiotics. How can bacteria develop new characteristics such as this when the daughter cells are always genetically identical to the parent cells? How does a daughter cell suddenly become resistant to an antibiotic that would have killed its parent? The answer to these questions lies with the diversity of the prokaryotes, their short 20-minute generation time, and the existence of plasmids.

Earth contains many different environments, and bacteria of varying species and strains have learned to live in every one of them. Over the short term, a few days or 10 years, the environment of a particular bacterium is not likely to change much, and for this reason clonal reproduction is not only adequate but it is also a wise choice. But over a very long period, thousands to millions of years, cells do change whether they clone themselves or not. Prokaryote DNA changes spontaneously at a rate of about one mutation per 300 chromosome replications. This amounts to about one mutation in a given lineage every four days. If these mutations are useful, the daughter cells will thrive and will pass them on to future generations. With a generation time of only 20 minutes, a useful mutation, when it does occur, can spread throughout a population very quickly.

But the genotype, or genetic composition, of a bacterium is not defined entirely by its main chromosome if it has a plasmid. Plasmids, like the main chromosome, carry genes that code for a variety of proteins that can destroy or neutralize an antibiotic. Plasmids are released into the environment when bacteria die and can be taken up by other bacteria in the immediate area. Thus if a bacterium that is sensitive to penicillin happens to acquire a plasmid carrying a penicillin-resistance gene, it can within minutes become resistant to the drug.

A clonal creature like a bacterium, striving for regularity and conformity in the short term but equipped with plasmids and a very short generation time, can change dramatically over a surprisingly brief period. With such flexibility, it is not surprising that prokaryotes continue to reproduce in this way. Free living, single-cell eukaryotes known as protozoans also reproduce asexually. Though their reproduction is through the more complex process of mitosis, the final result is the same: two daughter cells, genetically identical to each other. But many protozoans have evolved complex life cycles that alternate between asexual and sexual reproduction. The evolution of sexual reproduction among the protozoans was likely driven by their increased life span, and by the fact that sexual reproduction provides a way of reshuffling the daughter cell's genome so that, even in the absence of a mutation, the progeny are not simply clones of the parents.

The evolution of sexual reproduction split the living world into clones (somatic cells) and gametes (germ cells). In the case of an animal's body, all the cells are divided into two kinds: the germ cells and the somatic cells. Germ cells, located in the gonads, divide by meiosis, producing nonidentical daughter cells, or gametes, which are used for sexual reproduction. The somatic cells account for all the rest of the cells in the body. All of the somatic cells divide

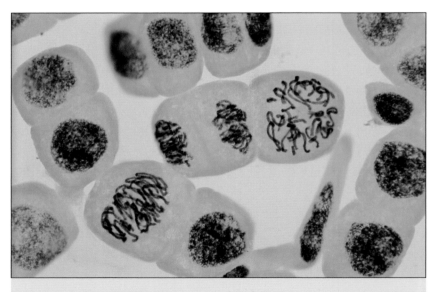

Onion *(Allium sativum)* root tip undergoing mitosis. The daughter cells produced in this way are clones of the original cell. Magnification: 200x. *(M. I. Walker/Photo Researchers, Inc.)*

mitotically and make up all of the tissues and organs, such as muscle, skin, blood, heart, and kidneys. Consequently, the animal grows through clonal reproduction of the somatic cells but reproduces sexually through the germ cells. Plants have a similar division of cell types. The cells making up the woody part of a rose bush divide asexually so the plant can grow, whereas the germ cells, located in the flower, allow the plant to reproduce sexually.

PLANT CLONES

Plants are sexual organisms, but their dependence on cloning as a survival strategy equals that of the prokaryotes. Indeed, the term *clone* was first introduced in 1903 by Herbert Webber, a botanist with the U.S. Department of Agriculture, to describe plants that are propagated by taking cuttings from a single plant. Thus in this context, a clone represents a pure line of plants, all of which are descended from a single self-fertilizing individual.

Plants have been cloning themselves for millions of years. A common method that plants use involves the formation of a runner, or modified stem, that grows some distance from the plant before it forms a second cloned copy of the original. This has great survival value in that it protects the plant from excessive grazing. An herbivore may eat the plant right down to the roots without destroying all of the cloned copies. Grass, strawberries, potatoes, and onions all clone themselves in this way. An alternative method relies on the hardiness of fragmented bits of a plant, produced by herbivores or gardeners. Given the right conditions, these bits or cuttings can form a mass of unspecialized cells called a callus, which can regenerate the entire plant.

Plants possess this remarkable regenerative capacity because of a special cluster of cells, called the meristem, which is located at the root tips, leaf nodes, and other growing points of the plant. The cells within the meristem are analogous to stem cells in animals. Plant meristems depend on their environment for growth cues: Meristems located under the soil will give rise to roots, and those above the ground will form leaves, stems, and flowers. Thus a favored tree or bush may be cloned simply by cutting off a lower branch and sticking the cut end into the soil to stimulate the growth of new roots (although gardeners often dust the cut end with root-forming hormone to speed things along).

ANIMAL CLONES

Many animals clone themselves for one reason or another. Indeed, some of them seem to have the regenerative talents of a plant. Most animal clones are either aquatic or terrestrial invertebrates, but reptiles and mammals also have some capacity for self-cloning.

Aquatic Invertebrates

Self-cloning is very common among marine and freshwater invertebrates. This is not to imply that these animals never have sex, since most of them do, but clonal reproduction has become a crucial part of their survival strategy. All of these animals are either sessile (attached to rocks or ground) or move very slowly. Two echinoderms, the sea cucumbers and the sea stars, are examples of marine invertebrates that reproduce sexually and by cloning themselves. Flatworms (planarian) and the hydra (cnidarian) are their freshwater counterparts. Clonal reproduction also occurs among terrestrial animals, such as the aphid, certain desert lizards, and even among humans.

Sea cucumbers look something like the vegetable they are named after, but ones that are covered in rows of shark's teeth and crowned with a mane of wormlike tentacles. This animal forages on the seabed, where it feeds on detritus and is affectionately referred to as an oceangoing vacuum cleaner. Being a slow-moving creature, it has to cope with fast-moving predators, a fact that has shaped both the sexual and asexual behavior of this animal. Sexually, sea cucumbers reproduce through a process called broadcast fertilization, whereby the males and females simply release their gametes into the water, where fertilization and development of the embryos and larvae take place.

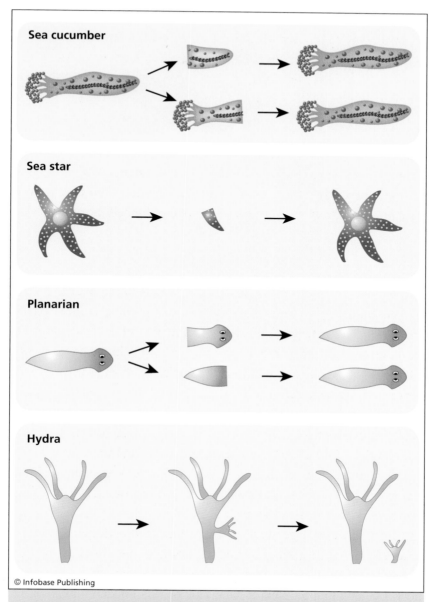

Invertebrate clonal reproduction. Sea cucumbers, sea stars, and planaria can all reproduce asexually by fission or fragmentation. The hydra can clone itself by forming a bud, which eventually separates and grows to adult size.

Sea cucumber *(Thelonata ananas)* on a sandy seabed. This species of sea cucumber, also known as a prickly redfish, feeds on detritus from the seafloor and may reach a length of up to 70 centimeters. *(SPL/ Photo Researchers, Inc.)*

Broadcast fertilization is a practical method of reproduction for sea cucumbers since they do not have to spend time finding members of the opposite sex. But there is a major problem with this strategy: The parents cannot protect their offspring, and fish love to eat echinoderm larvae. The sea cucumber tries to compensate by producing millions of larvae, perhaps enough to satisfy the predator's appetite while allowing a few to grow to maturity. If the predation stopped there, sea cucumbers could get by well enough with sexual reproduction alone, but unfortunately for them, fish and other predators such as the octopus also love to eat adult sea cucumbers, shark-tooth armor and all.

The survival of the cucumbers depends on the ability of the adults to produce an enormous number of larvae. Even a modest reduction in the size of the adult population can have serious consequences. The cucumbers solved this dilemma by evolving two forms of asexual reproduction: fission and fragmentation. When cucumbers reproduce by fission, they simply break in half, after which both pieces produce complete individuals that are genetically identical, and therefore are clones of each other. Fragmentation is essentially the same mechanism but one that is initiated by a predator. If a fish or an octopus takes a bite out of a sea cucumber but does not swallow the whole animal, that individual can regenerate itself from the piece that is left behind, as long as it represents at least half of the animal's body. Self-cloning has become such an important part of the cucumber's survival strategy that nearly half of the adults are produced this way.

Sea stars (or starfish) are also capable of asexual reproduction by fragmentation, but they seem to be more efficient at it than the cucumbers. If a predator such as an octopus attacks a sea star and eats all of it but a small portion of one arm, that piece of arm can regenerate the entire individual. People in the fishing industry first

The painted sea star *(Orthasterias koehleri)*. Found off the coast of Vancouver Island, British Columbia. *(Michael Patrick O'Neill/Photo Researchers, Inc.)*

observed the sea star's remarkable talent more than 100 years ago. Starfish were often caught in fishing nets, and it was the custom at the time to cut them up into several pieces before throwing them overboard. The fishers were hoping to reduce the numbers of starfish in their fishing grounds but abandoned the practice when they noticed it having just the opposite effect. Sea stars, like sea cucumbers, can also reproduce sexually through broadcast fertilization.

Freshwater flatworms can also reproduce through fission or fragmentation to offset losses and damage due to predation. These animals are popular subjects in many research projects aimed at gaining a better understanding of tissue regeneration, with a view to helping people who have lost an arm or a leg. Hydras, another freshwater invertebrate, reproduce asexually through budding. In this case the clone-daughter first appears as a small outgrowth, or bud, on the surface of the clone-parent, eventually pinching off to live independently. Hydras form buds continually, whether or not a

Light micrograph of the Cnidarian polyp *Hydra*. Other Cnidarians include the jellyfish, sea anemones, and corals. Cnidarians are represented by two body forms: the polyp, which is sedentary, and the medusa, which are free-swimming. *Hydra,* like all Cnidarians, are simple multicellular aquatic animals in which the mouth (upper center) is surrounded by tentacles that capture small items of food. *Hydra* can reproduce asexually by budding off a daughter polyp (as seen at left). *(SPL/Photo Researchers, Inc.)*

predator has damaged them, but this form of clonal reproduction serves the same adaptive role as fragmentation in sea cucumbers, sea stars, and planarians. If a predator bites off the entire top half of a hydra, the remaining piece of stalk can regenerate the individual. Predation on any of these invertebrates is analogous to the effect on grass of sheep or cattle grazing: As long as they do not consume the entire plant, roots and all, the remainder will grow back. The regenerative powers of grasses and other plants are familiar to us all, but marine and freshwater invertebrates have shown that simple animals have the same capacity.

For many of the aquatic invertebrates, learning to clone themselves was essential for survival. Echinoderms use it to balance the pressures from their predators to ensure an adequate production of larvae. Asexual reproduction is also important to some aquatic invertebrates as a mechanism of colonization. Hydras are generally sessile, or stationary, creatures, and reproducing asexually is a convenient way for them to colonize a new area. Currents may carry an individual far away from others of its kind, where, if it depended exclusively on sexual reproduction, it would take up the lonely, frustrated existence of an underwater Robinson Crusoe. Self-cloning allows reproduction of an entire population very quickly, and once this is done, many of these animals will revert to sexual reproduction.

Terrestrial Invertebrates

Terrestrial invertebrates, of which insects and spiders are the sole representatives, reproduce sexually, but this is not their only form of reproduction. Some, like the aphids, have a complex life cycle that includes both sexual and asexual reproduction. These insects are small (about 1/8 of an inch [2 mm] long), usually green or yellow in color, and are found feeding on nearly all indoor and outdoor ornamental plants, as well as vegetables, field crops, and fruit trees.

Aphids spend the winter as fertilized eggs attached to stems or other parts of plants. The young insects (or nymphs) hatch from

Aphids *(Acyrtosiphon)* being preyed upon by a ladybug *(Harmonia con-goblata)*. Aphids clone themselves through parthenogenesis. *(Nigel Cattlin/Photo Researchers, Inc.)*

these eggs and mature into wingless females called stem mothers. Males appear later in the year. Stem mothers reproduce by parthenogenesis (eggs and embryos are produced mitotically, without mating), and the eggs are held within their bodies until they hatch, so that nymphs are born alive. All offspring are female clones of the mother, which soon mature and begin to reproduce in the same manner. This asexual portion of the life cycle may last for more than a dozen generations. Eventually, some or all of the young aphids develop wings and migrate to other plants. As autumn approaches, bringing with it shorter days and cooler temperatures, a generation appears that includes both males and females. After mating, these females lay fertilized eggs to complete the cycle.

Aphids, like sea cucumbers and hydras, clone themselves, but their reason for doing so is quite different. When an aphid is caught by one of its predators, such as the ladybug, it is killed and consumed with no parts left behind, so there is no point in trying to exploit the properties of fragmentation. Instead, this little insect uses clonal reproduction to maximize the availability of food for its young. The stem mothers are, in effect, born pregnant so no time is wasted in a search for sexual partners, egg development, and so forth. As soon as the vegetation is in bloom, the aphid population is there, ready and waiting. And since most of the other insects reproduce sexually, there will be a brief period when the aphids have the fresh vegetation all to themselves, usually to the dismay of the family gardener or farmer.

Reptiles

Most vertebrates, whether aquatic or terrestrial, reproduce sexually, but there are some reptiles that prefer to clone themselves. When animals began roaming the Earth, many of them learned to live in extremely harsh but stable environments. Some species spent millions of years fine-tuning their anatomy and physiology so they could live in a desert or on the ice floes of Antarctica. Among this unusually hardy group of animals is the whiptail lizard, living in the deserts of the southwestern United States. To look at them, one would think whiptails are very ordinary lizards, yet on closer

Great Basin whiptail lizard *(Cnemidophorus tigris)*, Pyramid Lake, Nevada *(Karl H. Switak/Photo Researchers, Inc.)*

inspection two things become evident: First, they all look remarkably alike, and second, they are all females. Whiptails, like aphids, reproduce by parthenogenesis, but their life cycle does not include a sexual stage, nor do males ever appear in the population. How this came to be is not clear. Perhaps the number of whiptails dropped so low that the males and females had trouble finding one another. Somehow females appeared in the population that could reproduce asexually and eventually the male line died out. Presumably, these females were exceptionally well adapted to their environment so that the loss of sexual reproduction was no disadvantage.

However, relying entirely on asexual reproduction is a practical strategy only when the environment is stable. Deserts rarely revert to wetlands, and the whiptails are betting they never will. However, most environments are not so stable, and for this reason other creatures that clone themselves, like sea cucumbers or aphids, retain the ability to reproduce sexually in order to guard against the possibility of entering a genetic dead end and the threat of imminent extinction that comes with it.

Mammals

Mammals, including humans, their farm animals, and their pets use sex to reproduce, and in the natural environment there are no exceptions. But this is not to say that mammals never clone themselves; they do, but the progeny are called twins instead of clones. Identical twins occur when the two-cell embryo splits into two separate cells, or blastomeres, both of which develop into a normal adult, with each being the clone of the other.

Scientists would now like to extend this natural process to the cloning of adults. The reasons for doing so are sometimes vague, but in the case of farm animals, the intention is to produce herds of genetically identical individuals very quickly, or to use cloning as a way to produce transgenic animals that function as pharmaceutical factories or serve as a convenient source of vital organs. Those wishing to clone human adults usually cite a desire to replace a loved one or to create copies of gifted individuals.

Needless to say, the prospect of scientists cloning human adults has stirred up a great deal of controversy. Humans are sexual creatures who take a dim view of any attempt to short-circuit the process. The source of this attitude is sure to be complex, but the human psyche seems to have an intuitive grasp on nature's love for

Twins *(Andresr/Shutterstock, Inc.)*

variability and the connection between sexual reproduction and intelligence. It is no accident that the most intelligent creatures on Earth are mammals: creatures that not only reproduce sexually but also spend a great deal of time nurturing and caring for their young. Human emotions and intelligence can be traced to the nurturing that is typical of all mammals. The sense of suffering and the pain that is felt when a loved one is hurt or killed is a big part of what makes us human. Those emotions were there when human ancestors picked up rocks to drive off a predator, and when scientists developed the first diphtheria vaccine in the hopes of saving dying children. These elements of the human mind have served us well for more than a million years, but the great fear is that human cloning could cripple it all in less than a century.

2

The History of Animal Cloning

Animal cloning began in an attempt to understand embryonic development. Plants and animals, in honor of their very distant ancestors, begin their lives as individual single cells. The cell is called an egg or an oocyte, and when the oocyte is fertilized, a developmental program is activated that produces an organism made up of many millions, sometimes billions, of cells. But the creation of a multicellular creature is not just a matter of an oocyte dividing many times to produce a great bunch of cells. Instead, embryogenesis is a combination of cell division and differentiation. Cell division increases the number of cells, while differentiation transforms those cells into many different kinds. By the time a human infant is born, the child's body consists of several billion cells, representing 200 distinct types that form his or her flesh and blood.

Cellular differentiation is clearly evident in the physical transformation of the embryo throughout development. Embryonic

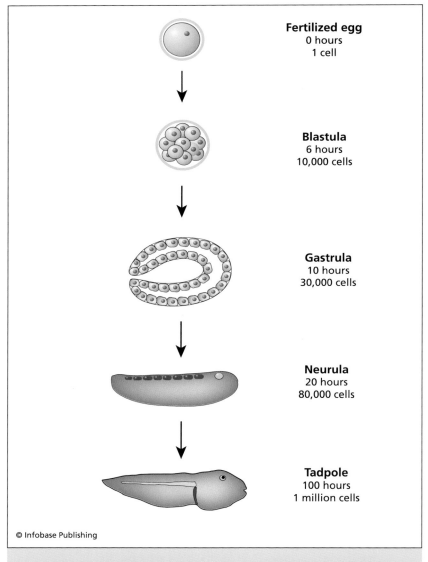

Embryonic development in the frog. The fertilized egg divides to produce a hollow ball of cells called a blastula, which invaginates to form a gastrula. Development of the nervous system and a segmented spinal column produces a neurula. The tadpole eventually forms an adult frog after going through a nonembryonic stage called metamorphosis.

development is similar in most animal species and is divided into three major stages. The first stage is the formation of a blastula, a spherical hollow ball of embryonic cells known as blastomeres. The second stage occurs when the blastula invaginates to produce a gastrula, which defines the body axis and establishes future identities of the cells and tissue layers. The final stage begins with the formation of a nervous system and, in the case of vertebrates, the segmented spinal column. At this stage the embryo is called a neurula, and the process is known as neurulation. The final form of an embryo also depends on organogenesis, or the formation of organs such as the heart and kidneys, and morphogenesis, whereby similar tissues are molded into different structures, such as an arm and a leg.

EMBRYOS INSPIRE THE FIRST CLONING EXPERIMENT

While Louis Pasteur, a 19th-century French microbiologist, was using his microscope to study bacteria, other biologists were using their instruments to study embryonic development, and they quickly realized that cellular differentiation posed a major riddle: How can a single cell, the oocyte, with one genome differentiate into so many different kinds of cells? If all the cells have the same genes, why don't they all look and act alike? In 1885 August Weismann, a German zoologist/embryologist, proposed that embryonic development was associated with a diminution, or loss, of genes. Brain cells become brain cells because they have lost the genes specifying liver or skin but retain genes that specify neurons. Weismann further suggested that diminution began with the first cell division in which the left blastomere retained genes for the left side of the embryo and the right blastomere had only genes for the right side. With the first division of the egg, all of the cells lost their totipotency; that is, they could no longer give rise to a complete individual.

Two other German embryologists, Wilhelm Roux and Hans Dreisch, set out to test Weismann's theory shortly after it was proposed. Roux collected fertilized eggs of the frog, *Rana esculenta;* as soon as an egg divided, producing a two-cell embryo, he destroyed one of the blastomeres by poking it with a hot needle. Roux reasoned that if the two blastomeres retained the same genetic information, the undamaged one would develop normally, but if diminution occurred, as Weismann predicted, it would not. Each time Roux performed his experiment the embryo failed to develop normally, and Weismann's theory seemed to have been confirmed. Hans Dreisch was not convinced, however, and in 1894 he decided to try a similar experiment using sea urchin embryos. Instead of destroying one blastomere, the way Roux had done, he shook the two-cell embryo until it separated into two cells, both of which developed normally. Dreisch concluded that Weismann was wrong and that Roux's experiments were flawed: Perhaps destroying one blastomere damaged the other or prevented it from developing normally. But Dreisch was unable to repeat his experiment using frog embryos, as they would not shake apart, and he could find no way of separating the two blastomeres without damaging one or both of them.

Hans Spemann, a German biologist with a passion for embryology, was finishing his Ph.D. when Dreisch was conducting his experiments. Although Dreisch could not separate amphibian blastomeres, Spemann developed a simple and elegant method to separate the cells without damaging either one. After collecting fertilized salamander eggs, he very carefully, and with infinite patience, looped a strand of a hair taken from his newborn son between the two blastomeres and gently tightened the noose until the two cells came apart. Both of the blastomeres went on to produce normal tadpoles.

Spemann concluded that nuclei at the two-cell stage are totipotent. Weismann's diminution, as Dreisch had shown, did not occur. But, Spemann wondered, was it possible that diminution occurred more gradually? Are nuclei at a more advanced stage still totipotent? To answer these questions, Spemann performed a second test of totipotency, which is also the first cloning experiment ever conducted.

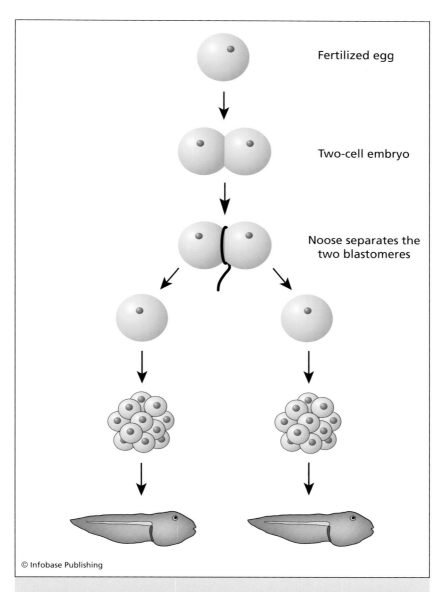

Fertilized egg

Two-cell embryo

Noose separates the
two blastomeres

© Infobase Publishing

Experiment to test totipotency. A noose was used to separate a
two-cell embryo into two blastomeres. Development proceeded
normally in both embryos, proving that nuclei at the two-cell stage
are totipotent.

Dr. Hans Spemann, a 19th-century German embryologist who performed the first animal cloning experiment using amphibian embryos. *(NLM/ National Institutes of Health)*

Again Spemann collected fertilized salamander eggs, but this time he did not wait for them to divide. Instead, he quickly tied a loop of baby hair around the egg and gently tightened the noose to produce two blastomeres, one with a nucleus and one without (an enucleated or blank cell). He kept the noose tightened until the nucleated blastomere divided to produce 16 cells, at which time he loosened the noose just enough to let a nucleus from the 16-cell embryo pass into the blank cell. Quickly he tightened the noose and kept it drawn until the 16-cell embryo separated from the one-cell embryo, and to his delight, both went on to develop into normal tadpoles.

Spemann was a very thorough scientist who devoted his entire professional life to the study of embryos. Throughout his career, he conducted many experiments, some of which earned him, along with his brilliant student, Hilde Mangold, the Nobel Prize in physiology and medicine in 1935. He was amazed, and to some extent overwhelmed, by the complexity and level of integration that he observed in developing embryos, but the question of totipotency was

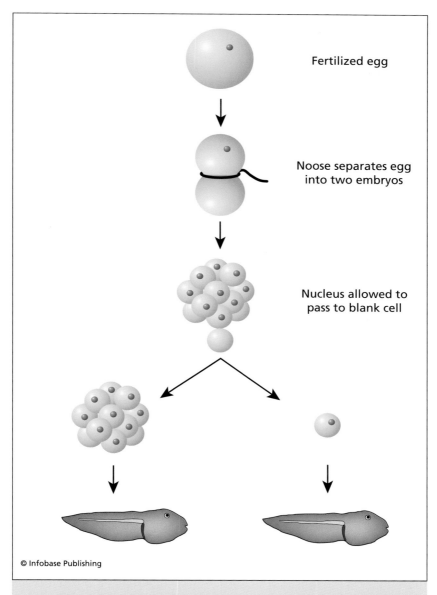

Fertilized egg

Noose separates egg into two embryos

Nucleus allowed to pass to blank cell

The first cloning experiment. A noose was tied around a fertilized salamander egg to produce one cell with a nucleus and one without (blank cell). At the 16-cell stage, the noose was loosened to allow a nucleus to pass into the blank cell, after which the 16-cell embryo was separated from the one-cell embryo.

always on his mind. In 1938 he wrote *Embryonic Development and Induction,* in which he wondered if cell nuclei remained totipotent throughout the life span of the adult. What would happen, he asked, if a nucleus from an adult cell were transferred into an enucleated egg? He did not call it "cloning" but referred to it as a "fantastical experiment." Spemann was excited about this experiment, but he could see no way of conducting it, and indeed, it would take more than 50 years before anyone could find a way to do it. When they did, Weismann's theory was laid to rest, once and for all.

CLONING FROGS IS A PARTIAL SUCCESS

Robert Briggs and Thomas King, his graduate student, cloned the first frog in 1952 at a research institute in Philadelphia. This was not quite the "fantastical experiment" envisioned by Spemann. Briggs and King obtained their nucleus from a gastrula, not an adult, but it was an important first step. Using extremely fine pipettes, King withdrew the nucleus from a frog's egg (oocyte), in this case *Rana pipens,* then injected a nucleus from a gastrula into the now enucleated oocyte. The embryo developed normally up to the tadpole stage, at which time the experiment was declared a success even though the researchers had not waited for the tadpole to metamorphose into an adult. They repeated their experiment many times, eventually cloning 27 tadpoles from a total of 197 oocytes that had received a transplanted gastrula nucleus. They found, however, that their success rate dropped dramatically when they tried to use nuclei from a neurula, a later-stage embryo. Briggs and King eventually concluded that Weismann was at least partially correct. Nuclei from older embryos did not appear to be totipotent. Perhaps, they thought, the DNA was somehow rearranged during development so that the cells pass a point of no return. If true, this meant that it would never be possible to clone an adult.

John Gurdon, a British biologist at Oxford (currently Sir John Gurdon at the University of Cambridge), thought that the problem

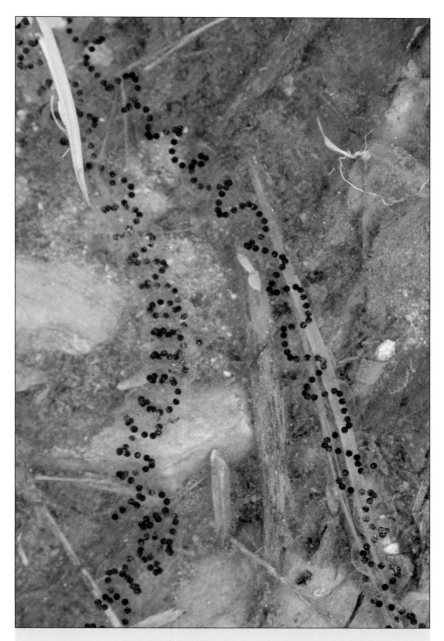

Strings of frog eggs *(Steffen Foerster Photography/Shutterstock, Inc.)*

Portrait of British geneticist Sir John Gurdon (b. 1933), professor of cell biology at Cambridge University and chair of the Wellcome CRC Institute for Cancer & Developmental Biology in Cambridge, United Kingdom. Educated at Eton and Christ Church, Oxford, Gurdon was elected a Fellow of the Royal Society of London in 1971. His research concerns the way genes control the development of specialized cells from rapidly dividing cells in vertebrate embryos. *(Jerry Mason/ Photo Researchers, Inc.)*

was not that cells lost their totipotency but that it was being repressed. The genes are all there, but the oocyte cannot use them. Cloning an adult would require reconditioning the adult cell nucleus so it could support embryonic development. Gurdon also suspected that the damage done to the oocytes, while having their nuclei removed, might have contributed to the failure Briggs and King encountered when trying to clone from older embryos.

But Gurdon was not interested in cloning an embryo—Briggs and King had already done that. Instead, he set out to clone an adult frog, and he chose to work on the African toad, *Xenopus laevis,* because the species has especially large, clear eggs. Clear eggs were important because rather than withdrawing the oocyte nucleus with a pipette, as Briggs and King had done, Gurdon destroyed it with ultraviolet (UV) radiation. He then collected epithelial cells from the intestinal tract of an adult toad and placed them in tissue culture. As soon as an oocyte was exposed to UV, it received another nucleus obtained from the cultured epithelial cells. In some cases, after the clone developed to the blastula or gastrula stage, its nuclei were isolated and injected into other oocytes in an attempt

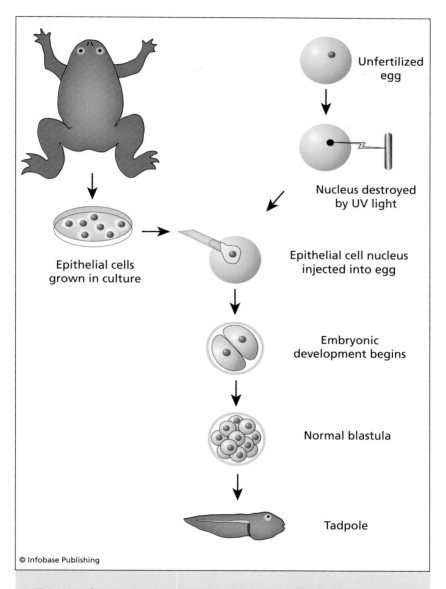

Unfertilized egg

Nucleus destroyed by UV light

Epithelial cells grown in culture

Epithelial cell nucleus injected into egg

Embryonic development begins

Normal blastula

Tadpole

© Infobase Publishing

Cloning a frog by nuclear transfer. Epithelial cells are collected from an adult and grown in culture. An unfertilized egg cell is collected and exposed to UV radiation to destroy its nucleus. A nucleus, with some cytoplasm surrounding it, is extracted from a cultured epithelial cell and injected into the enucleated egg. If successful, the clone will develop into a normal blastula and finally a tadpole.

The African clawed frog, *Xenopus laevis (Michael Redmer/Visuals Unlimited)*

to recondition them through another round of cloning. After several rounds of this treatment, it was assumed that the nuclei were reprogrammed and could support full development, right up to the adult stage.

Many of Gurdon's experiments led to the production of cloned tadpoles, a few of which metamorphosed into adult frogs. However, shortly after he published his results, other scientists discovered stems cells in the intestinal tract of *Xenopus,* casting some doubt on the outcome of the experiment. Stems cells are undifferentiated and account for about 2.5 percent of the cell population in the gut lining. If nuclei from these cells were used, Gurdon's experiment would be more like cloning an embryo rather than an adult. Moreover, Gurdon's success rate for obtaining cloned adults was about 2 percent, very close to the expected proportion of stem cells in his tissue culture samples.

Nevertheless, Gurdon's success, partial though it was, made it clear to most scientists that cells retained their totipotency and that it was only a matter of time before someone found a way to reawake a differentiated nucleus so that an adult animal could be cloned.

CLONING MAMMALS IS DECLARED IMPOSSIBLE

Gurdon's work was both exciting and exasperating. Cloning an adult could be done, many were certain of it, but so far no one had been able to do it. When discussions came around to the possibility of using nuclear transfer to clone a mammal, everyone seemed to think that it would be impossible. First, frog embryos develop in the water, so the mother frog stocks her eggs with everything the embryos will need to grow, and for this reason their eggs are very large, making them relatively easy to work with. In addition, because development of the embryo occurs outside the mother's body, frog eggs that are being prepared for a cloning experiment can simply be returned to the water for incubation, with few special precautions needed.

Mammalian embryos, on the other hand, get their nourishment from the mother through the placenta, so there is no need for the eggs to be stocked with food reserves the way frogs' eggs are. This is why a mammalian egg is so tiny, only 1/100 the size of a frog's egg. In addition, the placenta is derived from the trophoblast, an opaque cell layer that surrounds the embryo, making manipulations of the embryonic cells extremely difficult. The trophoblast also gives rise to the chorion, a membrane that surrounds the embryo, forming a safe, fluid-filled chamber in which development occurs. The placenta and chorion can develop only in a mother's womb. Mammalian eggs, after being manipulated in a cloning experiment, cannot simply be placed in a fluid-filled culture dish for the embryo to develop. Instead, they have to be implanted in the womb of a surrogate mother that will carry the embryo to term. All of these conditions made the cloning of mammals seem impossible.

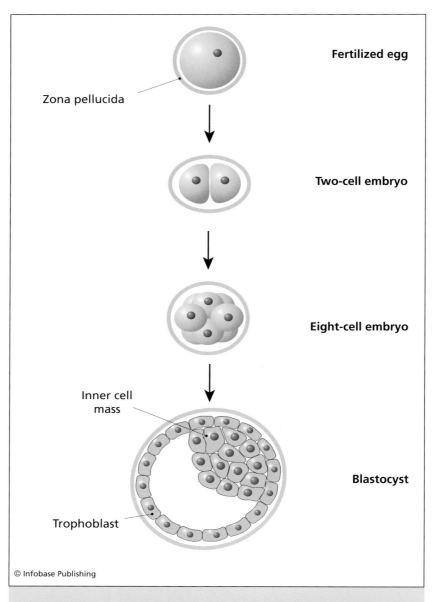

Mammalian embryogenesis up to the blastula stage. Mammalian embryos, unlike amphibians, are surrounded by nonembryonic cells that make up the zona pellucida and trophoblast, the latter giving rise to the placenta and chorionic membrane. The embryonic cells are in the inner cell mass.

But there are always scientists who enjoy attempting the impossible, and in 1981 Karl Illmensee and his associate Peter Hoppe reported cloning three mice. Again, this was not Spemann's "fantastical experiment," since Illmensee obtained nuclei from embryonic, not adult, mouse cells, but it was, nevertheless, a stunning achievement. Illmensee used the basic procedures for nuclear transfer, established in the earlier frog cloning experiments, as well as techniques for handling mammalian oocytes that were developed in the 1970s by Patrick Steptoe and Robert Edwards for in vitro fertilization (that is, fertilization in a culture dish) of human embryos.

Illmensee and Hoppe collected fertilized eggs from black mice and developing embryos from gray- and brown-colored mice. Nuclei were isolated from the embryos and injected into the eggs, after which the egg's original nuclei were removed using the same pipette. After the cloned embryos were constructed, they were allowed to grow in vitro for a few days before being implanted in the uterus of white surrogate mothers. Three apparently healthy mice were born. One was brown, and the other two were gray. The coat color provided an immediate confirmation that the genetic origin of these mice was the nuclei obtained from gray and brown embryos.

The real power of science lies in the fact that it is based on experimentation and the careful description of the experimental method, so other scientists can try to replicate the results. Experiments that cannot be replicated, or repeated with the same results, are of little use to anyone and cannot help us gain a better understanding of nature. Indeed, when scientists are unable to replicate an experiment, they tend to get rather grumpy about it and usually conclude that the procedure is faulty or that the scientists responsible for developing the experimental protocol are less than reputable: Perhaps they did not get the results they claimed.

This was the situation facing Illmensee and Hoppe soon after they published the results of their cloning experiment, for others tried to replicate their results but were unable to do so. Some scientists went so far as to assert that the results were not only fraudulent but that the cloning of mammals was biologically impossible.

CLONING FARM ANIMALS SETTLES THE DEBATE

Scientists, like everyone else, occasionally get the wind knocked out of their sails. Illmensee and Hoppe's cloning experiments were greeted with great enthusiasm, but eventually the careers of both scientists were ruined by the suspicion that their results were fraudulent. Not everyone believed this, however. Nor did everyone think that cloning a mammal was impossible; they believed in Mark Twain's observation that you cannot depend on your eyes when your imagination is out of focus. And indeed, in 1986, just five years after Illmensee's trouble began, Steen Willadsen, working in Cambridge, England, cloned a sheep from embryonic cells.

Willadsen, a veterinarian turned reproductive biologist, began by finding ways to freeze and store sheep embryos. This is important since many embryos are usually required for these studies, and it is necessary to collect as many as possible during the breeding season, after which they are stored until needed. After thawing some of his embryos, Willadsen transferred them to surrogate mothers, and eventually he was able to get healthy lambs and calves from embryos that had been frozen and stored.

He then decided to try a simple twinning experiment, using Spemann's method to separate a two-cell sheep embryo into two healthy blastomeres. But the procedure is not as straightforward with mammalian embryos as it is with amphibians. Splitting a two-cell mammalian embryo destroys the zona pellucida, without which the embryo cannot be reared in vitro. In Spemann's experiment the split blastomeres were placed in pond water for development to continue. With mammalian embryos it is necessary to incubate them in vitro for a day or two before implanting them in a surrogate mother. The in vitro step is carried out in the fallopian tubes of a rabbit, either in situ (still intact in the rabbit) or isolated and kept alive in a culture dish. In either case, without the protection of the zona pellucida, the rabbit's immune cells quickly destroy the embryo. Willadsen solved this problem by coating the separated blastomeres in a gelatinous substance called agar before placing them in the fallopian tubes. Nutritive molecules, being supplied by the fallopian tubes, can pass through the agar, but the cells of the immune system cannot. After three to four days the individual blastomeres, now grown to 16-cell embryos, were transferred to a surrogate mother, where they developed into healthy twins.

Having perfected his technique with twinning experiments, Willadsen cloned three sheep from an 8-cell embryo and then extended his experiments to dairy cows, which he cloned from more advanced, and more highly differentiated, embryos consisting of 120 cells. These experiments set the stage for Spemann's "fantastical experiment," the cloning of a sheep named Dolly from adult cells. It was not until Dolly's birth in 1996 that Weismann's theory was finally laid to rest. Genes are not lost during development but simply repressed, and thus embryonic development occurs through a process of differential gene expression; that is, turning genes on or off in a way that is specific to each cell type. All the cells in an adult's body express the basic housekeeping genes, but liver cells do not express brain-specific genes, and neurons do not express liver-specific genes.

3

A Clone Named Dolly

When Dolly was born on July 5, 1996, Hans Spemann's fantastical experiment was finally accomplished. But Spemann was not on Ian Wilmut's mind when he set out to clone sheep. Most biologists, including Wilmut, knew about Spemann and the work of Illmensee and Willadsen, but scientists often end up going down a particular research trail simply because it is the only one open at that moment in time. In some cases they may have been hired to solve a particular problem and, in trying to deal with it, ended up on a path that happens to run parallel to the research efforts of other scientists.

Research is, after all, an exploration of the unknown, one that plays out like an old-fashioned detective story, where each bit of information becomes a clue that leads to the next piece in the puzzle. Scientists, like all good bloodhounds, simply follow the nose. From time to time they also consult their intellect, and if they are wise, they hope for a bit of luck. Nonscientists are often surprised to hear this—they assume a researcher approaches a problem in a very organized, systematic fashion: Form a hypothesis, conduct the experiment, analyze the data, draw the conclusions, and paint the final picture. Deductive reasoning plays a big part in all of this, but as likely as not, it is intuitive insight and plain old dumb luck that save the day. Scientists generally shy away from the phrase "dumb luck," preferring to call it serendipity.

Serendipity played a major role in the birth of Dolly. Ian Wilmut, working at the Roslin Institute in Scotland, (now Sir Ian Wilmut at the University of Edinburgh) did not set out to prove the biology community wrong in its assertion that the cloning of mammals was biologically impossible, nor did he try to fulfill Spemann's dream. He was simply trying to find a better way to produce transgenic farm animals, and along the way he and his team accidentally hit

Roslin Institute, Edinburgh, Scotland, the research center where the British researchers Ian Wilmut and Keith Campbell created Dolly the sheep in 1997. Dolly was the first animal cloned from an adult cell. The institute's main areas of research are in genomics (the study of the genetic code), transgenics (inserting genetic material from one species into another), biotechnology, and the breeding, welfare, and behavior of animals. *(Volker Steger/Photo Researchers, Inc.)*

Scottish scientist Ian Wimut leans on the bust of German scientist Paul Ehrlich after he was awarded the Paul Ehrlich and Ludwig Darmstaedter science prize in Frankfurt, Germany, in 2005. *(Michael Probst/AP)*

upon the importance of G_0, a special stage of cell division. Without that piece of the puzzle, Dolly would have remained a dream.

DOLLY IS CLONED FROM AN ADULT CELL

The totipotency of cell nuclei declines as an embryo develops into an adult. Before Dolly's birth, the question of whether it is possible to reprogram a fully differentiated nucleus had never been resolved. So the birth of Dolly came as quite a shock to scientists around the world because the nucleus that was used to produce her came from a fully differentiated mammary gland cell that was originally obtained from a six-year-old Poll Dorset ewe.

Poll Dorsets are a common Scottish breed of sheep that are all white. Another popular breed is the Scottish Blackface, which is very similar to a Poll Dorset, except that it is larger, has horns and, of course, has a black face. Both breeds figured prominently in the experiments that led to Dolly. A Poll Dorset has a life span of about 12 years, so the cell that gave rise to Dolly was not only from an adult, but from a middle-aged one at that. Dolly, being derived from a Poll Dorset nucleus, is herself a member of this breed.

The general scheme for cloning Dolly involves placing a nucleus from an ovine mammary gland epithelial (OME) cell into an enucleated egg obtained from a Scottish Blackface. The nuclear transfer procedure Wilmut and Campbell used was originally introduced by Steen Willadsen. The karyoplast (the cell donating the nucleus) is injected into the space between the zona pellucida and egg cell. The karyoplast and the cytoplast (the enucleated egg) are then fused together with an electric current. This is a much gentler procedure, compared to injecting the nucleus into the egg by poking another hole in the egg's membrane (the first hole was made when the egg's chromosomes were removed). Once development begins, the embryo is encased in agar and incubated temporarily in the oviduct of a Blackface (not shown in the figure), after which it is transferred to the oviduct of the final surrogate mother, also a Blackface, which carries it to term.

Wilmut and his team constructed a total of 277 embryos, of which 29 developed to the blastocyst stage in the temporary surrogate. These blastocysts were removed from the agar and transferred to 13 Blackface ewes, one of which became pregnant and gave birth to Dolly. With only one out of 277 embryos going full term, it is a wonder the experiment worked at all. The scientists could tell at a glance that the experiment had worked, since Dolly was clearly a white-faced Poll Dorset and not a Scottish Blackface. Despite the obvious differences between the surrogate mother and Dolly, extensive DNA tests were conducted to prove that Dolly's genome came

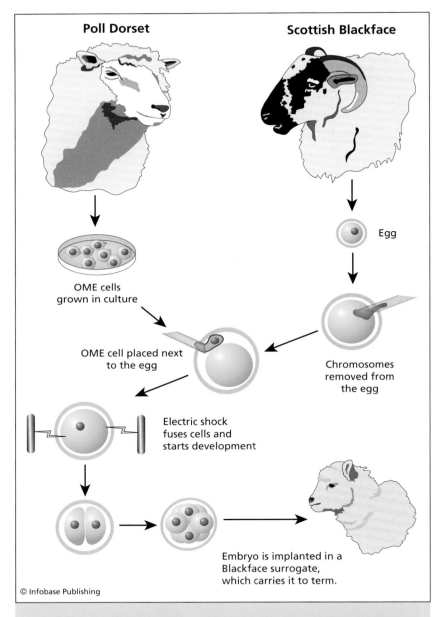

Poll Dorset

Scottish Blackface

Egg

OME cells
grown in culture

OME cell placed next
to the egg

Chromosomes
removed from
the egg

Electric shock
fuses cells and
starts development

Embryo is implanted in a
Blackface surrogate,
which carries it to term.

© Infobase Publishing

How to clone a sheep. The Poll Dorset provides the nucleus, which is obtained from cultured ovine mammary gland epithelial (OME) cells. The blackface provides the egg, which is subsequently enucleated. If the cloning process is successful, the clone will look like a Poll Dorset.

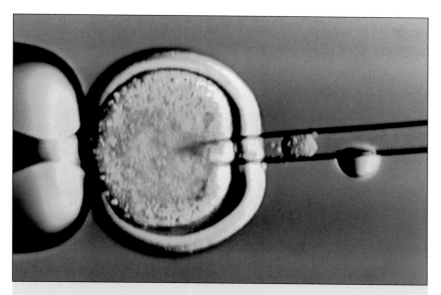

Light micrograph of a sheep egg being injected with a cell nucleus
(James King-Holmes/Photo Researchers, Inc.)

from the culture of OME cells, and that she was indeed a clone of
one of those cells.

THE IMPORTANCE OF BEING G_0

Why was Wilmut's team successful when so many before them had
failed? Although the procedure used to clone a frog appears to be
very similar to the one used to clone Dolly, there are in fact many
differences. The gentle fusion of the karyoplast to the cytoplast and
the coating of the embryo in agar for the pre-incubation period
were important innovations, but the crucial difference between the
Dolly experiment and all other previous cloning experiments is the
consideration Wilmut's team paid to the details of the cell cycle (the
cell cycle is discussed in chapter 10).

One of Dr. Wilmut's team members, Dr. Keith Campbell, a spe-
cialist in cell-cycle control mechanisms, realized that the chances
of successfully cloning a sheep would be much greater if the cells

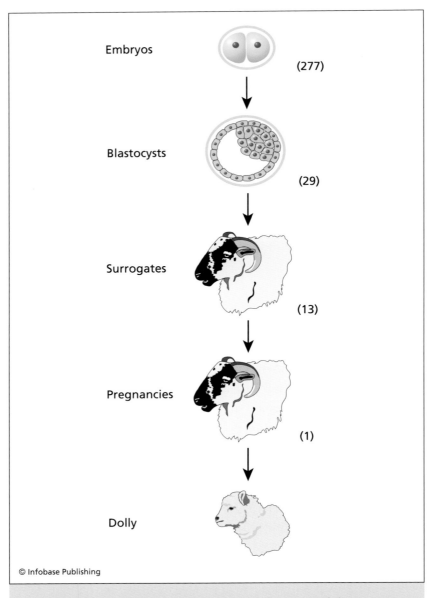

Embryos

(277)

Blastocysts

(29)

Surrogates

(13)

Pregnancies

(1)

Dolly

The Dolly experiment. Dolly was cloned from an adult mammary gland cell via the GOAT protocol. The difficulty of reprogramming adult nuclei is apparent from the very large number of embryos produced, from which only a single lamb, Dolly, was born.

Dolly, photographed at the Roslin Institute on February 25, 1997, when she was seven months old. *(Paul Clements/ Associated Press)*

being used as nuclear donors were in G_0. There are two reasons for this: First, the chromatin of a G_0 nucleus is especially susceptible to reprogramming; second, the nucleus is still diploid. If the cell has been allowed to pass through S phase and into G_2, the DNA has duplicated, producing a tetraploid nucleus. Failure is guaranteed if such a nucleus is transferred into an enucleated egg.

Mammalian eggs released at ovulation are in metaphase of meiosis II; that is, they have passed through meiosis I, and with the completion of meiosis II, will become haploid. When the sperm enters an egg, it stimulates the completion of meiosis II, activating development. An important part of activation is the joining of the egg nucleus with the sperm nucleus to reconstitute a normal diploid nucleus. This is the reason cloning experiments using nuclei from G_2 or S cells fail: The egg is expecting to begin development with a diploid nucleus but finds itself trying to deal with one that is tetraploid, or nearly so. Total confusion results, and the embryo dies.

Campbell devised a simple method for ensuring the cells used to obtain nuclei were in G_0. First, the cells were grown in culture, and then certain growth factors were left out when the culture medium was changed. Cells that were in G_1 left the cycle and entered G_0. Cells that were in S phase or G_2 either died or entered G_0 after completing their cycle. After a time it could be safely assumed that all of the cells were in G_0 and could be used as a source of donor nuclei. Initially, it was believed that G_1 and G_0 were equivalent, since the nucleus is diploid in either stage, but Campbell quickly realized that G_0 was not just a resting stage. Several lines of evidence provided by other scientists showed that this stage of the cell cycle was associated with subtle changes in chromatin structure, making the nucleus much easier to reprogram.

Campbell also considered the cell cycle stage of the oocyte and the possible effects it might have on reprogramming G_0 nuclei. All mammalian oocytes develop through meiosis I and stop at metaphase of meiosis II, at which point the duplicated chromosomes, held together at the centromeres, are lined up along the spindle. If they are never fertilized, they never complete meiosis. They are, in a sense, locked in a form of suspended animation, a condition that is controlled by maturation promoting factor (MPF).

MPF is responsible for triggering chromosome condensation and the breakdown of the nuclear envelope. MPF is, in turn, regulated by a molecule called CSF. When a sperm enters an egg, it triggers an influx of calcium ions into the cell. The calcium blocks CSF, leading to a drop in MPF activity. With MPF gone, the chromosomes decondense, the nuclear envelope reforms, and the cell completes meiosis II. Thus it is the influx of calcium that activates development, not sperm entry. Consequently, it is possible to add a nucleus to an egg without activating it, simply by carrying out the procedure in a solution that lacks calcium. In addition, adding a nucleus to an egg without activation would expose the nucleus to high levels of MPF, which could help reprogram the transplanted nucleus. These facts were used to design three cloning protocols, referred to as MAGIC, GOAT, and UNIVERSAL, all of which use G_0 nuclei.

MAGIC (Metaphase Arrested G_0-Accepting Cytoplast)

The karyoplast, the cell donating the nucleus, is fused to the cytoplast (the enucleated egg) in calcium-free solution. Four to six hours later, development is stimulated with another electric shock, this time in a solution containing calcium. The MAGIC protocol exposes the G_0 nucleus to the potential reprogramming environment provided by high MPF levels.

GOAT (G_0 Activation and Transfer)

In this case, fusion of the karyoplast and cytoplast occurs simultaneously with the electric shock. This procedure most accurately reflects normal conception. MPF levels begin dropping as soon as the cytoplast is activated, so the G_0 nucleus is exposed to high levels of MPF for only a brief moment.

Universal

An electric shock activates the cytoplast, and four to six hours later the karyoplast is added. Consequently, G_0 nucleus is never exposed to MPF, which will have disappeared by the time fusion occurs. This protocol is called "universal" because eggs without MPF were thought capable of accepting nuclei in any stage of the cell cycle.

Wilmut's team tested these protocols prior to the Dolly experiment, and they resulted in the live birth of two sheep, Megan and Morag. The birth of these two sheep marked the first time a mammal had been cloned from cultured cells; the cells used were obtained from sheep embryos that had been kept in culture for a month or two. Steen Willadsen had previously cloned sheep from embryonic cells but not from cells that had been placed in culture. The difference is important. Cloning from cultured cells is much more difficult because the cells have had a chance to differentiate, and their nuclei must be reprogrammed.

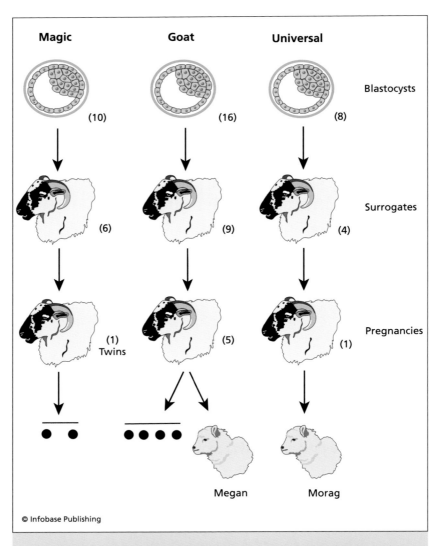

Magic   Goat   Universal

Blastocysts

(10)   (16)   (8)

Surrogates

(6)   (9)   (4)

Pregnancies

(1)   (5)   (1)
Twins

Megan   Morag

© Infobase Publishing

Three cloning protocols. The MAGIC, GOAT, and UNIVERSAL protocols were tested in a series of experiments that produced Megan and
Morag, the first mammals cloned from cultured, embryonic cells. The
number of embryos and fetuses at each stage are shown in paren-
theses. The black dots indicate the lamb was born dead, or died soon
after birth.

Dolly was cloned from an adult cell kept in culture for several months using the GOAT protocol. The choice of this protocol rested primarily on the fact that it produced the greatest number of pregnancies, even though it yielded only one live birth (Megan). The preliminary experiments involving Megan and Morag simply had too few embryos going to full term for a clear distinction to be made between MAGIC, GOAT, and UNIVERSAL. Theoretically, MAGIC should have been the best and UNIVERSAL the worst protocol. The GOAT protocol was a happy compromise in that it produced a live birth and exposed the transplanted nucleus to MPF for a time, brief though it was.

The careful attention to the details of the cell cycles of both the egg and donor nucleus cell is widely accepted as the crucial element in the Dolly experiment, but the difficulty of reprogramming an adult nucleus is evident from the large number of embryos that were produced, from which only one live birth, Dolly, resulted. With only one out of 277 cloned embryos carried to term, it is not surprising that the experiments of other scientists, who ignored the details of the cell cycle, failed, and drew the false conclusion that the cloning of mammals is biologically impossible. Cloning mammals is not impossible, just extremely difficult.

CLONING FROM CULTURED CELLS

Dolly was not just the first mammal cloned from an adult cell—she was also the first mammal cloned from adult cells grown in culture. Obtaining nuclei from cultured cells converts cloning from an interesting experiment to an extremely powerful method for producing transgenic animals. This was in fact Ian Wilmut's primary interest from the very beginning.

Transgenic animals are those that have had a foreign gene introduced into their genome by a process called transfection. Prior to Dolly's birth, the only method available for producing transgenic animals was to inject individual embryos with the foreign gene, after which the researchers had to wait for the birth of the animal before they could confirm the success of the experiment. Transfecting cells in culture is simpler, more effective, and more efficient. In some cases, it is only necessary to add the foreign gene to the culture medium, after which the cells will take it up and incorporate it into their genome. This is analogous to plasmid swapping, something that prokaryotes have been doing since life appeared on this planet.

Transfecting cells in culture offers a second, equally important advantage over previous methods: The cells may be tested to confirm the uptake and proper expression of the foreign gene before they are used in a cloning experiment. Some cells may incorporate the foreign gene but express it at levels too low to be of any use. By using standard molecular procedures, scientists can screen millions of transfected cells for the expression of the foreign gene. Once this is done, cells producing the desired amount can be isolated for cloning experiments. Using this approach, female sheep can be cloned that produce large quantities of valuable proteins in their milk. In 1997 Wilmut's team cloned a transgenic sheep named Polly that carries the human gene for blood clotting factor IX. This important protein can now be produced in large quantities to treat hemophiliacs (will be discussed in the next chapter).

DOLLY'S LIFE AND DEATH

By all accounts, Dolly was a healthy sheep right up to her death, at the age of six, on February 14, 2003. Dolly gave birth to six healthy lambs (one in 1998, two in 1999, and triplets in 2000). When she was born, many scientists feared she might develop a variety of medical disorders because all of her cells have abnormally short telomeres. A telomere is a simple DNA sequence that is repeated many times, located at the tips of each chromosome. Telomeres are not genes, but they are needed for the proper duplication of the chromosomes in dividing cells. Each time the chromosomes are duplicated, the telomeres shrink a bit, until they get so short the DNA replication

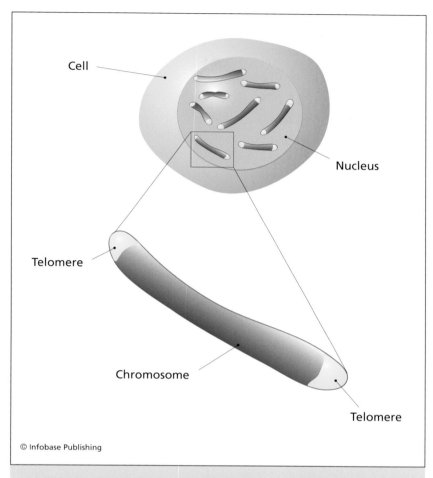

Telomeres. A telomere is a simple DNA sequence, located at the tips of each chromosome, that is repeated many times. Telomeres are not genes, but they are needed for the proper duplication of the chromosomes in dividing cells.

machinery can no longer work. This occurs because the enzyme that duplicates the DNA (DNA polymerase) has to have some portion of the chromosome out ahead of it. Much like a train backing up on a track, DNA polymerase preserves a safe distance from the end of the DNA so it does not slip off the end. Telomeres also provide a guarantee that genes close to the ends of the chromosomes have been replicated. DNA polymerase stalls automatically whenever it gets too close to the end of the chromosome, permanently blocking the ability of the cell to divide. When this happens, the cell is said to have reached replicative senescence. Telomere length decreases with age; the cell used to clone Dolly came from a six-year-old sheep and had been kept in cell culture for many weeks. Consequently, Dolly's genome was already middle-aged when she was born.

Wilmut's team analyzed Dolly's telomeres in 2000 and showed that they were indeed about 20 percent shorter than is normal for a Poll Dorset of Dolly's age. But the damaging effects of shortened telomeres on the health of a cell and the physiology of the organism are still highly speculative. In 2001 Dolly was reported to have developed arthritis in her left knee and hip joint. Arthritis is a common ailment in sheep, although it usually affects other joints. There is no way to know if the arthritis was related to the length of her telomeres or to the fact that she was a clone, simply because there are too few clones available for the information to be meaningful.

Other cloned animals do seem to suffer from a variety of medical problems. Dairy cows cloned in 2001 suffer from immune deficiencies. Two of three cloned Charolais calves, also cloned in 2001, died of an intestinal infection caused by a depressed immune system. The three calves, cloned at the California State University at Chico, were the only survivors among more than two dozen fertilized eggs planted in surrogate mothers. The success rate for the Dolly experiment was even lower and could also have been caused by problems with the immune system.

Researchers involved in animal cloning are actively monitoring their clones for subtle physiological abnormalities. Some abnormalities are likely to occur among the few cloned individuals that make it to adulthood. Scientists at the Roslin Institute estimate that a cloned fetus is 10 times more likely to die in utero than a fetus produced by normal sexual means. Moreover, cloning efficiency has barely improved over the years; it took 277 attempts to produce Dolly, and today the number is about 200. To date, scientists have cloned rabbits, sheep, horses, cats, mice, mules, dogs, and pigs. Typically, less than 10 percent of these clones survive to adulthood. Rudolf Jaenisch and his team at the Whitehead Institute for Biomedical Research in Cambridge, Massachusetts, examined the expression of 10,000 genes in cloned mice and found that nearly 4 percent of them were not being expressed properly as compared to natural-born mice. Such a high level of aberrant gene expression is almost certainly the cause of the low survival rate and the high rate of abnormalities that has been observed in cloned animals.

This state of affairs will not change until scientists gain a better understanding of nuclear reprogramming. When this happens, it may be possible to improve the success rate for cloning sheep from the current 1–3 percent to 20–30 percent. As the success rate improves, scientists expect that many of the clones will be as normal as lambs born by natural means.

4

Transgenic Clones

With current technologies it is possible to clone farm animals, such as sheep, goats, dairy cows, and pigs, that replicate human genes. Such clones are said to be transgenic, or genetically engineered, because they contain a gene, the transgene, from a different species. Although these animals have only one human gene (among about 20,000 of their own) they are still, technically, animal-human hybrids. The transgene usually codes for a protein that is medically important, such as clotting factors to treat hemophilia. In this case, the transgenic animal, always a female, produces the foreign protein in her milk, from which it is easily isolated.

Despite the relatively benign nature of transgenic husbandry, the general public tends to view this kind of research with suspicion and, sometimes, hostility. Cloning mammals for the production of transgenic creatures seems like something that could easily get out of hand. Such worries about dehumanizing scientific experiments have been with us for some time and frequently find expression in literature. H. G. Wells, a famous 19th-century British author, turned the production of human-animal hybrids into a science fiction horror story when he wrote *The Island of Doctor Moreau* (1869). The character Dr. Moreau is obsessed with the idea of producing human-animal hybrids, which he calls the beast-people. On a secluded island, in a laboratory known as the "house of pain," he creates cat-humans, wolf-humans, and other hybrids, all of which are physically monstrous. The beast-people eventually kill Dr. Moreau, leaving the reader with a lesson in morality that may best be summed up in the following way: Do not mess with nature or you will regret it.

H. G. Wells is often given credit for being a visionary, and his book is frequently mentioned in connection with the current production of transgenic animals. But Wells, like his contemporaries, did not foresee the emergence of biotechnology and its ability to mix genes from different species. Dr. Moreau produced his hybrids surgically (or through vivisection, as it was called in Wells's day) by mixing organs and tissues from various animals, all the time blissfully ignorant of the insurmountable problem of cross-species tissue rejection.

Comparing modern transgenic husbandry with the fictional work of Dr. Moreau is a stretch, to say the least, but the emotional force of the book and three subsequent movie versions (*Island of Lost Souls,* 1936, and *The Island of Doctor Moreau,* 1977 and 1996) leaves a powerful impression that is difficult to counter. These ideas came to the movies most recently with the release of *The Lord of the Rings* trilogy, by J. R. R. Tolkien, only here it is the evil Sauron who converts the beautiful elves into the loathsome orcs. Tolkien's trilogy was written in the 1930s, and he, like the rest of society, was strongly influenced by the character of Dr. Moreau. These very popular books and movies have influenced people to associate talk of hybrid animals with unpleasant images, but the difference between the beast-people of fiction and the transgenic animals currently being produced is profound. A transgenic sheep or goat looks like any other sheep or goat, and the transgenes they carry, rather than turning them into monsters, will help save the lives of millions of people worldwide.

BIOFACTORIES

Transgenic animals are called biofactories because they are able to mass-produce a substance that is harvested and sold, usually as a pharmaceutical product. Although in common usage, it is an unfortunate term in that it gives the impression the animals are treated like inanimate machines. There is, to be sure, an assembly-line quality to a transgenic farm, but no more so than on an ordinary dairy farm or cattle ranch. Farmers and ranchers have traditionally kept and maintained animals for food and clothing, and now they keep them to produce medicinal drugs.

Transgenic animals are cloned from females. The exception to this involves animals that are cloned for organ farming (discussed in chapter 5) or for the production of nonmedicinal products, such as spider's silk. Clones intended to produce medicinal products must be female in order to have the transgene expressed in the mammary gland. If the cloning procedure is successful, the adult clone's body will secrete the protein product into the milk, from which it is easily isolated. The cell-culturing stage of the standard animal-cloning procedure is the stage at which the transgene is added to the cells that serve as nuclear donors (karyoplasts).

The transgene, intended for the production of a useful drug, is always a gene that has been isolated from human cells. For example, sheep have been cloned that produce blood clotting protein IX, for treating hemophiliacs, by introducing the human gene for clotting protein IX into cultured sheep cells. Cells that take up the transgene and incorporate it into their nuclei are used to produce the embryo by the nuclear transfer procedure.

In most cases, the transgene is purchased from a pharmaceutical or biotechnology company that specializes in isolating and characterizing human genes. Characterization of the gene involves obtaining the complete DNA sequence for both the coding and controlling regions of the gene. The coding regions specify the structure of the protein product, while the controlling region, known as the promoter, determines when the gene is turned on or off. An important aspect of producing transgenic animals is ensuring the transgene is expressed appropriately. This requires swapping the gene's natural promoter with one that will allow expression of the gene in the target tissue.

Swapping promoters can be done using recombinant DNA technology. In the case of human clotting protein IX, its natural promoter ensures that it will be expressed in human bone marrow and nowhere else. If a scientist wishes to have this human gene expressed in the mammary gland of a sheep, it is necessary to swap the natural promoter with one that controls the expression of a sheep milk gene. One ingredient of sheep milk is a protein called β-lactoglobulin, a protein that helps stabilize the dominant milk sugar, lactose. Swapping the clotting factor IX gene promoter with an ovine (i.e., sheep) β-lactoglobulin gene promoter will ensure production of the clotting factor in sheep milk.

DRUGS FROM TRANSGENIC ANIMALS

There are currently five drugs being produced in transgenic animals: human clotting factor IX, human antithrombin, Alpha-1 antitrypsin, human antibodies, and human serum albumin. As mentioned above, clotting factor IX was the first to be produced, but antithrombin was the first to be approved by regulatory agencies for general medical use. These agencies, mainly the U.S. Food and Drug Administration (FDA) and the European Medicines Evaluation Agency (EMEA), have been slow to give their approval, partly because of the public's aversion to cloned products (including transgenic crops), but also because of the threat of an immune reaction to residual animal proteins that may contaminate the drug product. There is also a concern that the isolated drugs may contain animal prions (particles that cause scrapie and mad cow disease) and potentially dangerous viruses. Pharmaceutical companies have been working hard to improve the purity of their products and to overcome the public's fear of genetic engineering. This effort paid off in early 2009, when antithrombin was approved by the FDA.

Human Clotting Factor IX

Human blood, which is normally a liquid, is converted to a fibrous solid at the site of a wound. A blood clot, so formed, has several functions: It reduces blood loss; it covers the wound to prevent bacterial infection; and it provides a temporary patch until the cells repair the damage.

The formation of a blood clot is a complex process that involves at least a dozen enzymes and protein factors. The principal elements in the clotting process are the proteins prothrombin, thrombin, and fibrinogen. These proteins are modified in sequence, with the help of several clotting factors, to produce fibrin, the protein from which clots are made.

Hemophilia A is a disease characterized by a failure of the clotting process. It is caused by a mutation in the clotting factor VIII gene *(Hema),* located on the X chromosome, affecting one in 5,000 males. A second, much rarer form of this disease, identified in 1952, is hemophilia B. This form of the disease is caused by a loss of clotting factor IX. Hemophilia B is sometimes called Christmas disease after Stephen Christmas, the first patient diagnosed with this disease, and, for a time, factor IX was known as the Christmas factor. The chromosomal location of the factor IX gene is unknown. Both clotting factors, VIII and IX, are synthesized in the liver.

A famous carrier of Hemophilia A was Queen Victoria, who transmitted it, by the marriages of her children to the royal families of Germany, Spain, and Russia. Males are susceptible to this disease because they have only one X chromosome. Females, with two X chromosomes, are not likely to have a defective *Hema* gene on both chromosomes, and hence rarely show the symptoms of this disease.

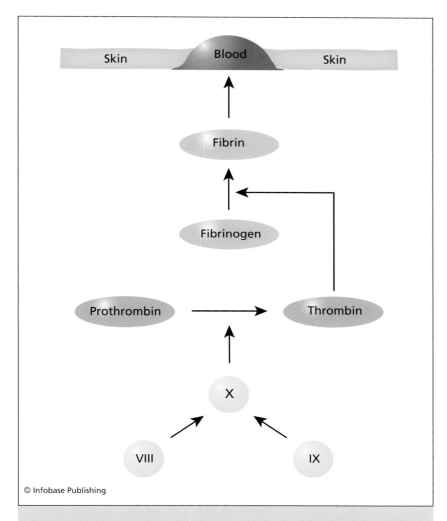

Formation of a blood clot. Two clotting factors (VIII and IX) activate a third (X), which stimulates conversion of prothrombin to thrombin. Thrombin then catalyzes the conversion of fibrinogen to fibrin to convert the drop of blood, collecting at a wound, to a solid clot.

Conventional treatment of Hemophilia A has involved regular transfusions of normal blood to replace the defective clotting factor, but this treatment is a major inconvenience and often leads to liver damage. Contamination of human blood supplies with the AIDS virus, and the resulting infection of many hemophiliacs in the 1980s, forced the development of alternative sources of factor VIII for replacement therapy, including antibody-purified factors and the production of factor VIII using DNA recombinant technology. These procedures produce safe, high-quality clotting factors but are extremely expensive.

Two methods are currently under development to deal with hemophilia: The first is gene therapy, whereby the gene for factor IX is injected into a patient suffering from this disease in the hope that it will provide the normal clotting factor. The second approach involves the production of transgenic cows or sheep that produce

Polly (left), and Dolly (right) are in their pen at the Roslin Institute in Edinburgh, Scotland, in December 1997. Polly and her clone-sister Molly (not shown) are the world's first transgenic animals. They each carry the human gene for blood-clotting factor IX, which may be used to treat hemophilia. Polly and Molly are clones of Dolly. *(John Chadwick/Associated Press)*

clotting factor IX in their milk. In 1997, the year after Dolly was born, Ian Wilmut's team was successful in producing several transgenic sheep expressing the factor IX gene. Research is now under way to produce factor IX transgenic cows and to assess the safety of this product. Transgenic cows are expected to produce a greater amount of factor IX than sheep do. An individual dairy cow will produce approximately 8,000 liters of milk per year containing an estimated 80 kilograms of factor IX. This is approximately 10 times the expected yield from a sheep. With a worldwide demand for factor IX exceeding half a ton per year, this difference is crucial.

Antithrombin

Antithrombin is a glycoprotein that inhibits blood coagulation. Although the name implies that it works only on thrombin, it is known to inhibit other coagulation enzymes, such as factors IX and X. Its ability to inhibit coagulation at multiple sites makes it one of the primary natural anticoagulant proteins and is frequently used to treat victims of heart attack and stroke.

A genetic disease called thrombophilia was described in 1965. This disease, characterized by excessive blood clotting, appears in two forms: Type I, which is an antithrombin deficiency, and Type II, which is caused by the production of defective antithrombin molecules. In either case, patients were treated with anticoagulants such as heparin or warfarin. Heparin is isolated from mucosal tissues (i.e., lungs, digestive tract) of slaughtered pigs and cows. Warfarin is synthesized from compounds originally isolated from moldy clover. Scientists discovered this compound when they noticed that cows feeding on moldy silage, consisting mostly of clover, died from excessive internal hemorrhaging because their blood lost its ability to clot. Heparin and warfarin, being nonhuman in origin, have unpleasant side effects when used for extended periods of time, and it is for this reason that transgenic human antithrombin has become such an important drug.

Alpha-1 Antitrypsin

This drug is used to treat cystic fibrosis (CF), a genetic disease that is extremely debilitating. CF is associated with the production of thick, sticky mucus that clogs the lungs, making breathing difficult and providing an environment that is susceptible to bacterial infection. Indeed, most sufferers of CF die of congestive lung failure, brought on by a bacterial infection, before the age of 30.

Cystic fibrosis is caused by a mutation in a gene that codes for a sodium chloride transporter, called CFTR, found on the surface of the epithelial cells that line the lungs and other organs. Several hundred mutations have been found in this gene, all of which result in defective transport of sodium and chloride by epithelial cells. The transporter can tolerate some amino acid substitutions, so the severity of the disease varies depending on the site of the mutation. A frequently occurring mutation does not cripple the transporter, but it does alter its three-dimensional shape and, as a consequence, the sorting machinery in the Golgi complex never delivers it to the cell membrane.

The loss of the CF transporter reduces the amount of water on the cell surface, thus increasing the density of the mucus layer, and is responsible for increasing the acidity inside the cell. The abnormal acid level leads to the production of a defective glycocalyx, which is unable to repel bacteria; as a consequence, a specific bacterium, *Pseudomonas aeruginosa,* is free to infect and destroy lung tissue. Conventional treatments are available that thin the mucus layer and kill *Pseudomonas,* but they are only partially successful. Patients suffering from CF must undergo regular treatment to dislodge the mucus in order to clear the airways. For them, life is a daily battle against suffocation.

The battle against cystic fibrosis, like hemophilia, is being fought on two fronts simultaneously: through the development of gene therapy to introduce a normal CFTR gene to the patient's cells, and the production of transgenic cows for the mass production of a protein called alpha-1 antitrypsin. This protein has been successfully to treat diseases affecting the lungs, such as cystic fibrosis and emphysema.

With every breath, large numbers of bacteria, bacterial spores, dust particles, and pollen are pulled into the lungs. The white blood cells of our immune system deal with these potentially dangerous particles by releasing an enzyme called neutrophil elastase (or, simply, elastase). This enzyme breaks down foreign particles but can also damage lung tissue if it is not properly regulated. The regulation of elastase is the job of antitrypsin. If too much elastase is released, antitrypsin binds to it, preventing the elastase from damaging lung tissue. Patients suffering from emphysema have an inadequate supply of antitrypsin, so their lungs are damaged by their own immune system, making it difficult for them to breathe. Similarly, children suffering from cystic fibrosis have a chronic lung infection, which stimulates the release of unusually large amounts of elastase. These patients, consequently, need greater than normal amounts of antitrypsin to protect their lungs from damage. The additional antitrypsin must be supplied to these patients in the form of a drug. Current estimates place the worldwide demand for antitrypsin, to fight lung diseases, at just more than one ton per year. The synthesis of this protein by transgenic animals is the only way to produce enough of this protein in the quality required for a medicinal drug.

Human Antibodies

Antibodies are proteins that assume a roughly spherical or globular shape (hence the word *globulin*) and are designed by the immune system to attack invading bacteria, protozoans, and viruses. Immunoglobulin is a mixture of human antibodies given to people with immune system deficiencies or as treatment for infections. It is normally derived from human blood; as a consequence, it is usually in short supply. In addition, antibodies for specific diseases can be obtained only from people who acquired the illness through

Two cloned Jersey calves each carrying a copy of a human antibody gene. These transgenic animals were produced at Hematech, Inc. These animals were cloned without destroying their own immune system. *(Dr. James M. Robl)*

the normal course of their lives. It is both unethical and illegal to expose people to a disease for the express purpose of harvesting antibodies. Transgenic cows, on the other hand, can be exposed to any number of infectious agents, and because of their size, they will produce large quantities of immunoglobulins.

There are no legal restrictions on the use of transgenic animals to produce human antibodies, but whether the procedure is ethical or not is up for debate. The complicating element here is the fact that the cows' own immune system will also produce antibodies, and these would be very difficult to separate from the human antibodies. The solution is to knock out (during the cloning procedure) the

cow's immune genes so only the human antibodies would be produced. How this will affect the cows' health is anyone's guess, but
in all likelihood they would have to live in a sterile environment: no
pastures, no trees, not even a walk through the barnyard.

Human Serum Albumin (HSA)

HSA is a major component of blood plasma and is involved in maintaining the balance of fluids between the blood and the tissues. It
also regulates the transport of amino acids, fatty acids, hormones,
drugs, and drug metabolites. Clinical uses include fluid volume replacement for patients suffering from shock and serious burns, fluid
administration during surgery, and for AIDS and cancer therapies.
HSA is also an important stabilizer that is added to antisera, such as
polio, cholera, and smallpox vaccines. HSA is, in itself, a powerful
incentive for obtaining human proteins from transgenic animals.
Worldwide demand for HSA exceeds 600 tons per year, with sales
of nearly $2 billion.

Transgenic cows are the only means by which the enormous
worldwide demand for HSA can be met. However, cow's milk contains an albumin that is very difficult to separate from its human
counterpart. Consequently, researches are trying to produce knockout transgenic cows that express HSA but lack the gene for their
milk albumin. This problem is similar to that already described for
obtaining human antibodies from transgenic cows, but in the case
of HSA, the knockout cows would retain a functional immune system and thus could be raised as ordinary dairy cows.

SPIDER SILK FROM GOATS

Drugs are not the only products obtained from transgenic animals.
Nexia Biotechnologies, located on a former maple-sugar farm in ru-
ral Quebec, has produced transgenic goats that express the gene for
spider's silk. As with the other transgenic products described, the
silk gene is expressed only in the mammary gland, so the silk protein

Transgenic goats produced at Nexia Biotechnologies in Quebec, Canada *(Sean O'Neal/Alamy)*

is released in the milk, from which it is easily isolated. Spider's silk is an extremely tough material that has five times the strength of steel and, according to Nexia's president and C.E.O., Dr. Jeffrey Turner, can be used to make fishing line and nets, bio-degradable surgical sutures, ultralight garments and sewing thread, tennis racket strings, body armor, and many other things.

Nexia's body armor has attracted the attention of the Pentagon, and with its financial backing, the company has set up a second plant in New York that will produce spider's silk under the trademark name of BioSteel. A bulletproof vest made from BioSteel would be just a bit thicker than nylon and practically weightless. Such a material was anticipated by Tolkien when he wrote *The Lord of the Rings:* "As tough as dragon scales and light as a feather," said Bilbo Baggins to his nephew Frodo, upon presenting him with a protective vest of near-magical properties made by the Dwarves from a mysterious material called mithril.

Unfortunately, the promise of BioSteel and other spider's silk products may never be realized. Dr. Turner resigned from Nexia in 2007 after the company had spent $67 million without bringing any of its products to market. Under the leadership of a new chairman and chief executive, the company is now diversifying into the oil and gas industry. The 40 transgenic goats produced by Dr. Turner's team are alive and well on a farm in Ontario and may be sold to another company interested in pursuing the work with BioSteel.

CLONING PRIZED ANIMALS

The transgenic products described above are sold in the market place, but the animals themselves are prized commodities. Researchers might want to expand these herds through cloning rather than conventional reproduction, or farmers and ranchers may be interested in applying transgenic technology to improve their poultry, pigs, or cows. The most direct approach is to select the animals that have the most desirable characteristics and then clone those animals to produce an entire herd of cows, cattle, or horses. The characteristics might include growth rate, muscle mass in beef cattle and poultry, milk volume in dairy cows, or resistance to disease.

Prized racehorses, mules, and favorite pets have all been cloned although not always with the results one might expect. In 2006, in what was billed as the first professional competition between clones of any kind, two mule clones of an undefeated champion, Idaho Gem and Idaho Star, finished third and seventh in the 20th annual Winnemucca Mule Race, held in the state of Nevada. Recent attempts to clone Thoroughbreds have been blocked by the Jockey Club, an organization that oversees horse breeding in North America. The official position of the group is that a race horse must be the result of a stallion's breeding with a broodmare. That is, no artificial insemination, no embryo transfers from one mare to another, and no cloning.

5

Organic Farming

Organ transplantation, involving the heart, lungs, liver, pancreas, and kidneys, is a powerful medical procedure that saves thousands of lives every year. The success of this procedure, however, has led to a great disparity between the number of people needing a transplant and the number of donated organs that are available. In 2009 more than 100,000 people were on a waiting list for an organ transplant in the United States alone; of these, only 28,465 received an organ, while more than 7,000 patients died because an organ could not be found for them. Despite a concerted effort on the part of the medical community to encourage organ donation, the number of people willing to do so has not changed since the 1990s.

In an effort to offset the grossly inadequate supply of organs, many scientists have studied the possibility of using organs obtained from pigs, which have hearts, kidneys, lungs, and pancreata very similar to those found in humans. Theoretically, pigs could be a ready source of these organs, thus making up the difference between patient need and donor availability. If such a plan worked, human organ donation could become obsolete.

However, the human immune system, designed to seek out and destroy foreign cells, has created a tremendous obstacle to the success of human-to-human (i.e., allogeneic) transplants and has so far rendered pig-to-human (i.e., xenogeneic) transplants a therapy of the distant future. Nevertheless, medical researchers agree that the future of organ transplants lies with xenotransplantation. Conventional allogeneic organ transplants, while only partially successful, are providing valuable information regarding tissue rejection and the many things that must be done to ensure a happy union between the transplant and the patient's immune system.

CONVENTIONAL ORGAN TRANSPLANTS

The kidney was the first organ to be transplanted, in the 1950s, and in 1967 the South African surgeon Dr. Christiaan Barnard performed the first successful heart transplant. This accomplishment was quickly followed by several other heart transplantations at Stanford University, in the United States. But the initial enthusiasm for kidney and heart transplantation was stifled by the sudden deaths of all of the first transplant patients, due to immune rejection of the grafted organs. During the 1970s, an immunosuppressant drug called azathioprine was introduced, which improved the survival of transplant patients, but rejection was still a major problem, with fewer than 40 percent of the patients surviving for one year after surgery. In 1983 a second, more powerful immunosuppressant, called cyclosporine, was introduced. This drug increased the one-year survival rate for kidney and heart transplant patients to more than 80 percent, opening the door to the successful transplantation of other organs, such as lungs, liver, and pancreata. Since the introduction of cyclosporine, additional immunosuppressants have been discovered, the most important of which are prednisone and tacrolimus. The role these drugs play in organ transplantation will be discussed in a later section.

In 2009 there were 27,399 Americans living with an organ transplant. This number reflects a nearly two-fold increase since 1992, when transplant data was first collected. Over this same time period, the total number of patients waiting for an organ transplant has more than tripled from 31,904 to 112,206. This large waiting list is due to the imbalance between the supply of organs and the growing demand over the past 18 years. Improved accessibility of some organs, such as the lungs, is due to a new deceased donor lung allocation policy that was implemented in May 2005. The allocation policy was changed from a system based on waiting times to one based on net survival benefit from transplantation and medical urgency (see the table on page 72).

Kidney Transplantation

The kidney is the organ most commonly transplanted; failure of the patient's original kidney is usually due to damage brought on by diabetes. In 1992, in the United States alone, 9,729 people received a donor kidney, increasing to 16,828 by 2009. The lack of donated kidneys to meet the demand for kidney transplants has worsened over the years. In 1992 the number of Americans on the waiting list for a kidney transplant was 22,063, increasing to an astonishing 89,140 patients by 2009, more than four times the number of available organs. The short-term success of kidney transplantation is impressive, with 96 percent of the transplant patients surviving the first year, dropping to 86 percent after five years (see the table on page 73).

Survival of the patient, particularly for a kidney transplant, is usually better than the survival of the grafted organ. Survival of the grafted kidney, at the one-year mark, is 92 percent, but organ survival drops sharply to 72 percent by the five-year mark, considerably lower than the survival rate of the patients. The difference in survivability between the patient and the grafted kidney is due to the fact that when the organ fails, the patient may receive a second kidney transplant, if a donor organ is available, or the patient may be kept alive with kidney dialysis. Thus it is the survival of the grafted organ that gives the truest picture of the overall success of organ transplantation. The heart, for obvious reasons, is the only case where survival of the graft and the patient correspond.

Cardiac Transplantation

Heart transplants are usually performed on patients who have sustained severe damage to their cardiomyocytes (heart muscle) because of blocked or clogged carotid arteries (the arteries that supply the heart with blood). These patients are generally middle-aged (50 to 60 years old), but there are also many infants and children who require a heart transplant due to congenital defects in the cardiomyocytes or gross anatomy of the heart or the heart valves.

Since the immunosuppressant cyclosporine was introduced in the 1980s, the number of heart transplants in the United States has increased from about a dozen in the late 1970s to 2,171 in 1992, an annual rate that remained relatively constant through 2009. As with the kidney, the number of heart transplants is limited by donor supply, since more than 3,000 patients were on the waiting list in 2009 (see the table on page 72). The number of heart transplants is also limited by the high cost of the procedure, currently estimated to be more than $300,000 (U.S.) for the first year. In addition, there is a $10,000 to $40,000 yearly cost for immunosuppressant drugs and follow-up procedures. These costs are particularly hard to meet in countries without medical insurance. The current one- and five-year patient survival rates are 87 and 71 percent.

The drop in the survival rate is due primarily to chronic rejection of the heart by the immune system. The daily diet of immunosuppressant drugs, prescribed for all transplant patients, inhibits the immune response, but does not abolish it completely. Day by day, the immune system launches small attacks on the foreign tissue, causing damage at the cellular level that over time leads to failure of the entire organ. Fifty percent of heart transplant patients show clear signs of this progression before the five-year mark.

When the transplanted heart is finally rejected, the patient's physician may recommend a second transplant, if an organ is available, but the one-year survival rate for a second transplant is very poor. Compounding the problem is the patient's poor health, brought on not only by a failing heart, but also by the immunosuppressants, which make it difficult for the patient to fend off several forms of cancer, in addition to a large number of infectious diseases.

Liver Transplantation

The biochemistry and physiology of the liver are extremely complex. This organ is charged with several important tasks: the removal of potentially toxic compounds from the blood; the production of substances, called bile salts, that are secreted into the intestine where they are involved in the digestion of fatty compounds; and the storage of amino acids and glucose (as glycogen). Detoxification of the blood is primarily concerned with the conversion of ammonia, which is lethal at high concentrations, to urea, a compound that is safely excreted by the kidneys. This process is carried out by a series of enzymes known as the urea cycle. Failure of this cycle is a common liver disorder that is often treated with transplant surgery. Other liver diseases that are treated with a transplant are chronic hepatitis, cirrhosis, and cancer. Many cases of liver cirrhosis are preventable, as they are brought on by excessive consumption of alcohol. There are also many inherited disorders of liver metabolism that primarily affect children, such as hemophilia and glycogen storage diseases, which are treated with whole or partial liver transplants.

Liver transplantation was pioneered in the 1960s at the University of Pittsburgh and in Cambridge, England. The procedure is now performed routinely in many medical centers throughout North America and Western Europe. In 1992, there were 3,036 liver transplants performed in the United States, with 5,789 patients on the waiting list. The number of liver transplants more than doubled by 2009, while those on the waiting list increased to more than 16,000. The one-year patient survival is nearly 87 percent, although organ survival drops dramatically to 64 percent after five years (see the table on page 73).

Lung Transplantation

Emphysema, a lung disorder frequently brought on by cigarette smoke, accounts for almost 60 percent of all lung transplants, with cystic fibrosis accounting for the remainder. Transplantation of the lung was first attempted in 1980, but the surgical procedures were not perfected until 1989, after which the number of transplants increased dramatically. Worldwide, the International Society for Heart and Lung Transplantation reported 900 lung transplants involving one or both lungs in 1994, followed by a dramatic increase to 8,997 transplants in 1999. In the United States, 535 lung transplants were performed in 1992, increasing to 1,660 in 2009. The ratio of wait-listed patients to transplants performed has improved since 1992. The one-year survival rate for lung transplant patients is 83 percent, but drops dramatically to 47 percent at the five-year mark (see the table on page 73).

Diseases affecting the lungs, such as emphysema, often affect the heart as well. Damaged lungs are incapable of supplying enough oxygen to keep the cardiomyocytes healthy. It is for this reason that patients suffering from lung diseases often require simultaneous heart-lung transplants; only 29 of these double transplants were carried out in 2009. The heart-lung transplant survival rate is poor: 67 percent at one year, dropping to 42 percent after five years.

Pancreas Transplantation

Failure of the pancreas is associated with the onset of type I diabetes. This disease is characterized by a failure of special cells in the pancreas, called beta cells, that produce insulin, a hormone that regulates the uptake of glucose by virtually every cell in the body. Diabetes often damages the kidneys, and for this reason, transplantation of the pancreas often follows, or is performed simultaneously with a kidney transplant.

Despite the link between kidney and pancreas failure, transplantation of the pancreas is rare, with only 64 cases reported in 1992, and 379 in 2009. This is because pancreatic failure can be treated for many years with insulin injections. Pancreas transplant patients show a one-year survival rate of nearly 93 percent, but the survival of the organ after five years is only 46 percent.

Organ Procurement

Obtaining organs for the many thousands of patients needing a transplant each year requires the coordinated effort of a virtual army of health professionals. In the United States, there are six principal organizations involved in organ procurement. Donor

THE NUMBER OF ORGAN TRANSPLANTS AND WAIT-LISTED PATIENTS IN THE UNITED STATES

ORGAN	1992		2009	
	TRANS-PLANTS	WAIT-LISTED	TRANS-PLANTS	WAIT-LISTED
Kidney	9,729	22,063	16,828	89,140
Heart	2,171	2,655	2,212	3,153
Liver	3,036	5,789	6,320	16,533
Lung	535	1,258	1,660	1,874
Pancreas	64	139	379	1,506
Total	15,535	31,904	27,399	112,206

Source: Organ Procurement and Transplantation Network.

SURVIVAL OF TRANSPLANT PATIENTS
AND TRANSPLANTED ORGANS
IN THE UNITED STATES

ORGAN	1 YEAR		5 YEAR	
	PATIENTS	ORGANS	PATIENTS	ORGANS
Kidney	96.2	92.0	86.5	72.5
Heart	87.1	86.4	70.7	69.5
Liver	86.4	82.7	71.4	63.6
Lung	83.2	81.7	47.4	46.5
Pancreas	92.6	76.8	77.4	45.6

Table values are percentages. The data was compiled from information provided by the Organ Procurement and Transplantation Network for 2009.

organs are obtained by 59 Organ Procurement Organizations (OPOs), which provide organs to 287 organ transplant centers. The OPOs are under the direction of governmental agencies, such as the Centers for Medicare and Medicaid Services (CMS) and the Health Resources and Services Administration (HRSA). The HRSA also funds the Scientific Registry of Transplant Recipients (SRTR), which maintains an organ transplant database and information center. Every OPO is a member of the Organ Procurement and Transplantation Network (OPTN), which is maintained by the United Network for Organ Sharing (UNOS). The rules for organ allocation, set by OPTN and UNOS, are computerized to enhance the speed, efficiency, and fairness of matching a donor organ with the nearly 100,000 patients currently registered with OPTN. The fairness of the distribution rules is especially important given the chronic shortage of organs. As already mentioned, several thousand people die every year in the United States while waiting for an organ. Thus the decisions made by OPTN and UNOS regarding

ORGAN TRANSPLANT ORGANIZATIONS IN THE UNITED STATES

NAME	ABBREVIATION
Organ Procurement Organization	OPO
Centers for Medicare and Medicaid Services	CMS
Organ Procurement and Transplantation Network	OPTN
United Network for Organ Sharing	UNOS
Health Resources and Services Administration	HRSA
Scientific Registry of Transplant Recipients	SRTR

Donor organs are obtained by 59 Organ Procurement Organizations (OPOs) that provide organs to 287 organ transplant centers. The OPOs are under the direction of governmental agencies, such as the Centers for Medicare and Medicaid Services (CMS) and
the Health Resources and Services Administration (HRSA). Every OPO is a member of the
Organ Procurement and Transplantation Network (OPTN), which is maintained by the
United Network for Organ Sharing (UNOS). The rules for organ allocation, set by OPTN
and UNOS, are computerized to enhance the speed, efficiency, and fairness of matching a donor organ with one of the more than 100,000 patients currently registered with
OPTN. The HRSA also funds the Scientific Registry of Transplant Recipients (SRTR), which
maintains an organ transplant database and information center.

who gets an organ and who does not mean life for some but death
for many others (see the table above).

IMMUNE REJECTION OF ORGAN TRANSPLANTS

A molecular forest, called the glycocalyx, covers the surface of every cell and has a central role in the process of matching tissues for
transplant operations. The trees in the cell's forest are glycoproteins and glycolipids that have "trunks" made of protein or lipid
and "leaves" made of sugar. These molecular trees are embedded
in the cell membrane much like the trees of Earth are rooted in
the soil.

The exact composition of the glycocalyx varies with each individual, much in the way an earth forest located at the equator is different from one located in the Northern Hemisphere. The human immune system uses the spatial arrangement of the exposed sugar groups to decide whether a cell is foreign or not. Thus the glycocalyx is like a cell's fingerprint, and if that fingerprint does not pass the recognition test, the cell is destroyed or is forced to commit suicide. Immunologists refer to the glycoproteins and glycolipids in the glycocalyx as cell-surface antigens. The term *antigen* arises from the fact that cell-surface glycoproteins on a foreign cell can generate a response from the immune system that leads to the production of antibodies capable of binding to and destroying the foreign cell.

An extremely important pair of cell-surface glycolipids is known as the A and B antigens. These glycolipids occur on the surface of red blood cells and form the ABO blood group system that determines each individual's basic blood type. The A and B antigens are derived from a third antigen, called H, which all individuals possess. Blood type A is produced by the A gene, which codes for a glycosyl transferase that adds an N-acetylgalactosamine to the H antigen. Blood type B is produced by a different transferase that places a galactose molecule on the H antigen. Some individuals have both A and B transferases and thus are said to have blood type AB. Individuals with blood type O have neither transferase. In North America, blood types A and O dominate, with A occurring in 41 percent of the population and O in 45 percent. Blood types B and AB are rare, with B occurring at a frequency of 10 percent and AB at only 4 percent.

An individual who is blood type A forms antibodies against the B antigen and therefore cannot receive blood from a type B individual, but he or she can receive blood from type O individuals. Similarly, a type B individual cannot receive blood from someone with blood type A but can receive it from someone who is type O. Individuals who have blood type AB can receive blood from individuals

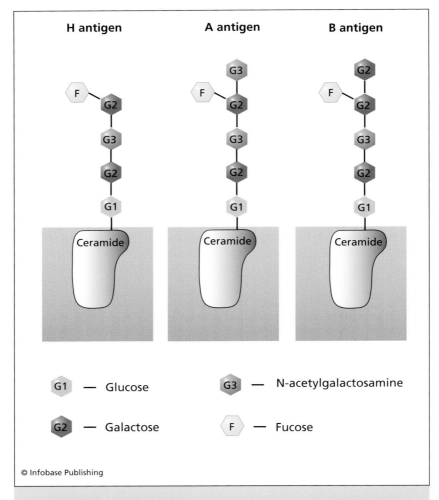

The ABO antigens on the surface of red blood cells. All individuals have the H antigen. In addition, 41 percent of North Americans have the A antigen, 10 percent have B, 4 percent have both A and B, and 45 percent have neither. The latter group is said to be type O.

who have blood types A, B, or O, and therefore such individuals are called universal recipients. On the other hand, people with blood type O can receive only type O blood since they will form antibodies against both A and B antigens. While individuals with type AB blood are universal recipients, individuals with type O blood are called universal donors because their blood may be given to anyone without fear of invoking an immune response.

The importance of blood type with respect to organ transplantation is best illustrated by the case of Jesica Santillan, a 17-year-old girl who required a heart-lung transplant to correct a congenital lung defect that also damaged her heart. On February 7, 2003, physicians at Duke University Hospital in Durham, North Carolina, replaced Jesica's heart and lungs without checking the blood type of the donor. Jesica was blood type O, but the donor was type A. Jesica's immune system rejected the mismatched organs, and she lapsed into a deep coma soon after the operation was completed. In a desperate attempt to correct the mistake, Jesica's surgeons replaced the mismatched heart and lungs with organs obtained from a type O donor, but it was too late. Jesica had already suffered severe and irreparable brain damage, and on February 22, 2003, she died.

As critically important as they are to the success of transplant surgery, the A and B antigens are only two of many thousands of cell-surface antigens that play a role in the rejection of foreign tissue. A second major group of antigens, called the human leukocyte antigens (HLA), may in fact number in the millions. These antigens are glycoproteins that cover the surface of virtually every cell in the body, not just leukocytes; they are called leukocyte antigens simply because that was the cell from which they were originally identified. When faced with this level of complexity, transplant surgeons have had to content themselves with matching only five or six of the most common HLA antigens between the recipient and donor. This, of course, leaves many mismatched antigens, but it seems that some antigens elicit a much stronger immune response than others, an effect that is likely quantitative in nature. That is, a million copies of antigen X will catch the attention of the immune system much more effectively than would 10 copies of antigen Y. By matching the dominant antigens, surgeons hope to avoid what is called the hyper-acute immune response, which leads to the immediate destruction of the transplanted organ and death of the patient. It was a hyper-acute response, brought on by a mismatch of dominant antigens, that killed Jesica Santillan. Matching dominant antigens does not mean the transplanted organ is compatible, only that the patient has a good chance of surviving the first year. Beyond that, the immune system begins a slow chronic attack on the remaining mismatched antigens, leading to eventual failure of most transplanted organs. The slow chronic attack is responsible for the poor five- and 10-year survival of transplant patients previously cited.

THE HUMAN IMMUNE SYSTEM

All immune systems are designed to protect an individual from invading microbes, particularly bacteria and viruses. Such a system does not understand the difference between a bacterium and a cell associated with a transplanted organ; as far as the immune system is concerned, both are foreign and need to be destroyed. Full success with organ and tissue transplants may be possible someday, but it will take a thorough understanding of our immune system and the methods it uses to fight invading cells. Equipped with that knowledge, scientists may be able to retrain the immune system to accept

(opposite page) White blood cells. These cells are divided into three major categories: granulocytes, lymphocytes, and monocytes. Granulocytes have a distinctive lobular nucleus, granulated cytoplasm, and all are phagocytic (eat cells, viruses, and debris). Lymphocytes have a smooth morphology with a large round or kidney-shaped nucleus. B lymphocytes are nonphagocytic but produce antibodies. T lymphocytes and natural killer (NK) cells coordinate the immune response and can force infected cells to commit suicide. Monocytes are large cells with an irregular shape. All monocytes are phagocytic and are large enough to engulf whole bacteria and damaged or senescent body cells.

transplanted organs—or at least to find a way to shield those organs from attack—to prevent their ultimate destruction.

The human immune system is composed of a large group of white blood cells that are divided into three major categories: granulocytes, monocytes, and lymphocytes. Granulocytes have a

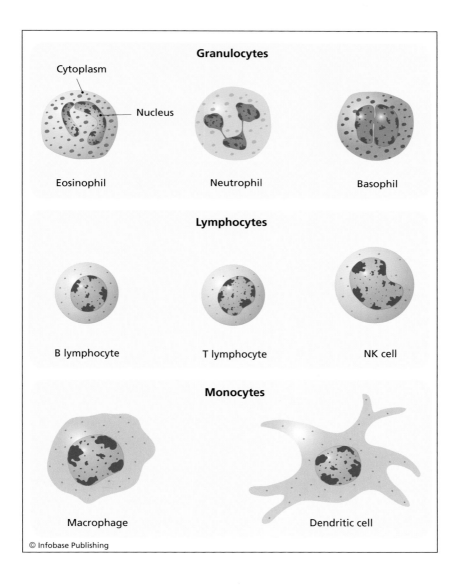

© Infobase Publishing

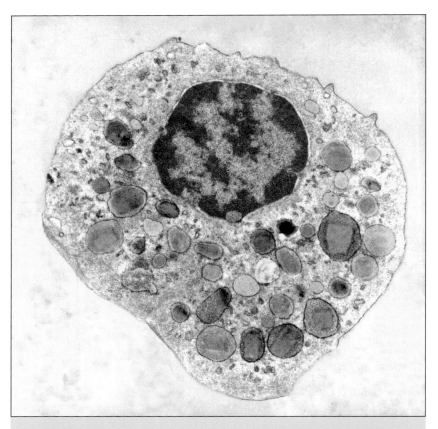

Human polymorphonuclear eosinophil *(BSIP/Photo Researchers, Inc.)*

distinctive, lobular nucleus, and all are phagocytic. Monocytes are large phagocytic cells, with an irregularly shaped nucleus. The largest monocytes, the macrophages, can engulf whole bacteria as well as damaged or senescent body cells. Lymphocytes have a smooth morphology and a large round nucleus. T lymphocytes and natural killer (NK) cells deal primarily with coordinating the immune response and with killing already infected body cells. B lymphocytes are nonphagocytic; they deal with an invading microbe by releasing antibodies.

Phagocytosis of an invading microbe by granulocytes and monocytes represents a first-line defense, called the innate response. All animals are capable of mounting this kind of defense. Activation of the lymphocytes leads to a more powerful, second line of defense, called the adaptive response, which is found only in higher vertebrates and is initiated by monocytes, specifically, dendritic and Langerhans cells. These cells, after engulfing a virus or bacteria, literally tear the microbe apart and then embed the pieces, now called antigens, in their membrane. The antigens are presented to lymphocytes, which become activated when their receptors bind to the microbial antigens. Activated B lymphocytes secrete antibodies specifically designed for that particular microbe. Activated T cells and NK cells attack the microbe directly but are primarily concerned with locating and killing infected body cells.

The T cell receptor is aided in the process of activation by a large number of coreceptors, called CD1 through CD120. CD4 and CD8 are commonly involved in mediating the activation of T cells by monocytes. The abbreviation "CD" stands for cluster of differentiation, meaning the coreceptor aids in the differentiation of the T cells. These coreceptors were originally identified by different groups of researchers using several hundred different antibodies. Eventually, they realized that many of the antibodies, referred to now as a cluster, were identifying the same coreceptor. Once activated, T cells recruit other T cells by secreting special, lymphocyte-specific growth factors called interleukins. More than 30 different interleukins have been identified, and they are referred to as IL-1 through IL-30.

The adaptive system can remember a pathogen long after it has been removed from the body. This is why a specific bacteria or virus cannot make us sick twice. Once infected, humans develop a natural, lifelong immunity. It is also possible to immunize ourselves against many diseases by injecting a crippled version of the pathogen, or specific antigens from a pathogen, into our blood-

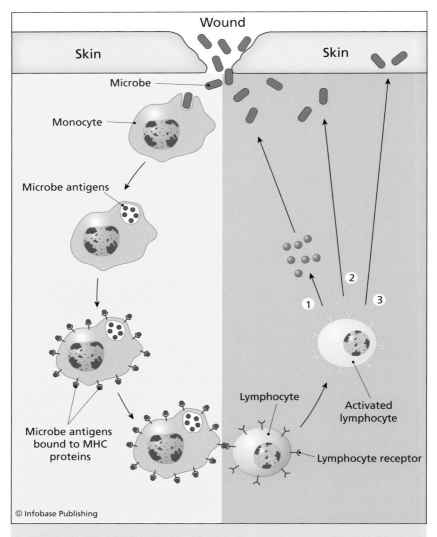

Innate and adaptive immune response. Phagocytosis of invading microbes is called the innate response. In higher vertebrates, microbe antigens, bound to special monocyte surface proteins called the major histocompatibility complex (MHC), are then presented to lymphocytes. Contact between the lymphocyte receptor and the antigen activates the lymphocyte and the adaptive response, consisting of a three-prong attack on the microbe and microbe-infected cells.

stream. This concoction of bits and pieces from a pathogen, called an immunizing serum, activates the adaptive response, leading to a lasting, though not always lifelong, immunity against the disease. It is the adaptive system that is responsible for the rejection of a transplanted organ; immunosuppressants, given to all transplant patients, are effective because they cripple this part of the human immune system.

SUPPRESSING THE IMMUNE SYSTEM

Blocking the immune response after transplant surgery is important, even in those cases where the major antigens have been matched. Prior to effective immunosuppressive therapy, transplant patients were lucky to survive the first few weeks following surgery. The current therapy is based on a collection of drugs and hormones that partially block the adaptive response, leaving the innate response largely intact. Immunosuppressants currently in use are azathioprine, cyclosporine, tacrolimus, glucocorticoids, and antibodies.

Azathioprine

This drug was first used in the 1970s to improve the one-year survival of heart and kidney transplant patients and is a molecule closely related to purines (important components of DNA and RNA nucleotides). Because of its similarity to purines, azathioprine can block both DNA and RNA synthesis. Activation of the adaptive immune response depends on the reproduction, through mitosis, of white blood cells; therefore, azathioprine is an effective immunosuppressant. Many patients, however, are especially sensitive to this drug and often develop serious side effects leading to damaged kidneys, jaundice, and anemia.

Cyclosporine

This compounds is a fungal peptide that specifically blocks transcription of mRNA for many of the interleukins, thereby inhibiting

T cell proliferation. The main side effect with this drug, as with azathioprine, is nephrotoxicity (i.e., damage to the nephron, the blood-filtering component of the kidney). In the case of a kidney transplant, it is often difficult to distinguish a rejection episode from cyclosporine-induced damage.

Tacrolimus

This is a fungal compound that has the same mode of action as cyclosporine, but the side effects are not as severe. However, while this drug has a lower nephrotoxicity than cyclosporine, it has a greater tendency to induce diabetes mellitus. Because diabetes is more easily treated than kidney damage, this drug is regarded as less toxic overall and is beginning to replace cyclosporine.

Glucocorticoids

A class of steroid hormones produced by the adrenal cortex called glucocorticoids has been used as effective immunosuppressants. A synthetic glucocorticoid called prednisone blocks the release of the interleukins IL-1 and IL-6, thus interfering with the activation of the adaptive immune response. This hormone is most effective when used in conjunction with either cyclosporine or tacrolimus. Extensive use of prednisone has severe side effects, most notably impairment of wound healing (including surgical incisions) and heightened predisposition to infection. Success with this hormone has been achieved with an alternate-day course of treatment.

Antibodies

Research is currently under way to produce antibodies that bind to and inactivate the CD coreceptors located on T cells. Different subpopulations of T cells express different CD molecules. Consequently, the use of tailor-made antibodies could provide a highly specific method for suppressing only a portion of the immune response, thus minimizing serious side effects.

ARTIFICIAL ORGANS

Artificial hearts and kidneys have been available since the 1970s and have been useful in maintaining seriously ill patients while they wait for a transplant or for new medical procedures that might restore their organs to health. Artificial kidneys have changed little over the years, but artificial hearts have improved considerably.

Artificial kidneys are called dialysis machines and are about the size of a small student's desk. The patient's circulation is diverted through the machine by two catheters, one carrying blood to the machine from an artery, and a second that returns the purified blood to the patient, through a vein in the leg. Patients with severe kidney damage can expect to be connected to a dialysis machine for an hour or more, several days a week.

The first artificial hearts were also large external machines that the patient was connected to. In the 1980s an American physician named Robert Jarvik introduced the first implantable artificial heart, the Jarvik-1, a device about the size of a real heart. In 1982 a team led by William DeVries of the University of Utah implanted an improved model, the Jarvik-7, into a patient named Barney Clark, who was not eligible for a transplant and was not expected to live for more than 30 days. Although the Jarvik-7 was small enough to be implanted, its power source was a large external air compressor that was a great hindrance to the patient's mobility. A second, and even more serious disadvantage of the Jarvik-7 was the excessive turbulence that it generated, which led to the formation of many blood clots. Blood clots are extremely dangerous because they can plug fine capillaries in the brain, causing a stroke, and they can plug the fine tubules in the kidney (the nephrons), leading to severe kidney damage and, ultimately, multiorgan failure. Barney Clark died from a severe stroke and kidney damage 112 days after receiving the Jarvik-7.

Abiomed Incorporated, a company that has been developing biomedical equipment for many years, introduced a much-improved implantable mechanical heart in 2000. Their mechanical heart, called the AbioCor, has two main advantages over the Jarvik-7. First, it does not require a bulky external power source but instead is run by a small battery pack that the patient wears on a belt around the waist. Second, the design includes a smooth flow chamber to reduce turbulence and the occurrence of blood clots. A major limitation of this heart is its large size, which limits prospective recipients to men with a large thoracic volume. The U.S. Food and Drug Administration (FDA) approved the AbioCor for clinical trials on January 30, 2001, and by February 2003, physicians at the University of Louisville's Health Science Center, in Danvers, Massachusetts, had

The AbioCor, an artificial heart produced by Abiomed, Inc. *(Dara Jacobsen/Abiomed, Inc.)*

fitted eight patients with one of these hearts. The maximum survival time of nearly two years attained by one of the patients was a dramatic improvement over the record of the Jarvik-7. However, for the remaining patients, survival was still measured in days (from 54 to 150 days), not years.

In September 2006 the FDA approved the AbioCor for commercial use under a Humanitarian Device Exemption (HUD). A HUD is defined by the FDA as a device that is intended to benefit patients by treating a disease that affects fewer than 4,000 individuals in the United States per year. This exemption is intended to encourage the development of experimental devices that are currently used as a last resort but show promise in the future. Abiomed is also working on the next generation of their mechanical heart, the AbioCor II, which is 35 percent smaller than the original and is expected to last for five years. Because of its smaller size, the AbioCor II can be implanted in both men and women and may be ready for clinical trials in 2010. Although this is a great improvement over the original, these devices still cannot compete with the results obtained for transplants of real hearts.

FUTURE PROSPECTS

A mechanical heart, no matter how well designed, is no match for the real thing. But real hearts, donated for transplant surgery, are in short supply. A seemingly ideal solution to this problem is to use hearts from farm animals, particularly from pigs, because they have human-sized organs. The catch to all of this, of course, is the human immune system: Without being suppressed, it does not allow an allograft (human organ transplant), and if confronted with a xenograft (animal organ transplant), the immune systems launches an all-out attack on the grafted tissue, known as a hyperacute response. Retraining the immune system to accept a xenograft is for the time being out of the question. But it may be possible to genetically engineer donor pigs so they lack the glycosyltransferases that produce the cell-surface antigens. An alternative is to produce transgenic pigs that express human cell-surface antigens. This is equivalent to producing a human-like glycocalyx on the surface of pig cells. In either case, the human immune system would treat the pig's heart as though it were an allograft, not a xenograft. The organ would still be attacked, as any unrelated, human-to-human transplant would be, but the attack is controllable with immunosuppressive therapy. This would solve the organ supply problem, and the patient's outlook for long-term survival would be much better than it would be with a mechanical heart.

To this end, researchers in the United States, Europe, and Japan have cloned transgenic pigs expressing human cell surface antigens and "knockout pigs" that lack the gene for α-1-galactosyltransferase. These animals improve the success of xenotransplantation, but many tests must be performed before clinical trials can begin.

6

Therapeutic Cloning

Throughout the 1990s, while Steen Willadsen and Ian Wilmut were laying the foundations for a procedure to clone mammals, other scientists were studying a special kind of cell called an embryonic stem (ES) cell. ES cells are blastomeres that are isolated from very young human embryos, no more than a few days old. Other kinds of stem cells can be found in the bone marrow and in the basal layers of the skin, where they serve to regenerate those tissues as they wear out. These cells, because they are usually isolated from adult tissues, are known as adult stem (AS) cells. Many scientists believe ES cells have a greater plasticity (i.e., a greater ability to form different kinds of cells) than AS cells, and thus are better able to treat a wide assortment of disorders such as spinal cord trauma and neurological disorders such as Parkinson's and Alzheimer's diseases.

Dolly the sheep was cloned as part of a research program that was designed by Ian Wilmut to produce transgenic animals. These animals, carrying and expressing human genes, could then be used to produce an unlimited supply of medically important compounds. Although effective, drug-based medical therapies have a limited scope and are usually intended to supplement a biochemical deficiency without curing the disease. Because of this, scientists have shifted their attention to cell-based therapies. Diseases such as leukemia, kidney failure, or cardiovascular disease are treatable through standard tissue (bone marrow) or organ transplants. These therapies can be effective, but the transplants usually come from donors that are not genetically identical to the patient and, consequently, the transplanted tissue or organ is attacked by the patient's immune system. The rejection of foreign tissue is known as graft versus host disease (GVHD). The only option for the time being is to keep the patients on immunosuppressants to slow down the rejection process. Immunosuppressants work well for the first few years, but eventually the transplant is destroyed.

With the cloning of Dolly, scientists saw a way to treat a multitude of diseases with ES cells without the fear of GVHD. In addition, organ transplants would become obsolete since the stem cells could be used to repair the damaged organs without replacing them. All of this could be done by cloning the patient, harvesting the stem cells from the embryo, and then using those cells to treat that same patient. ES cells can differentiate into many different kinds of cells, and in so doing, repair damaged tissues or organs in the body. Since the stem cells are derived from the patient, they are genetically identical and would not invoke an immune attack. For example, if a patient has a spinal cord injury, scientists could treat it by injecting stem cells into the injured area where they will differentiate into neurons and, it is hoped, repair the damage. If the stem cells are obtained from a generic lab culture, they will not be compatible with the patient's immune system and would induce GVHD. If the patient were cloned, the resulting embryo would be a source of immune-compatible cells that could be used without fear of rejection.

This kind of medical therapy is known as therapeutic cloning, an experimental procedure that has some potential, but is also highly contentious. In the minds of many, therapeutic cloning is unethical because the harvesting of the stem cells results in the death of a human embryo (in practice, the death of many embryos per patient). Thus this procedure creates a human life that has no future and is destined to be killed for its cells. Therapeutic cloning is also a difficult legal issue owing to the fact that countries around the world have already agreed to ban reproductive cloning. But if hospitals are allowed to clone patients for eventual therapy, it will be difficult, if not impossible, to guarantee that some of those embryos are not implanted into a surrogate mother and carried to full term.

HISTORICAL BACKGROUND

Therapeutic cloning depends on many scientific discoveries that occurred over the past 120 years. In the late 1800s biologists equipped with high-resolution compound microscopes and a few histochemical techniques were having tremendous success with the identification and treatment of many bacterial diseases. Robert Koch, a German country doctor, proved that anthrax, a fatal disease of cattle and humans, is caused by a bacterium, which he named *Bacillus anthracis.* Shortly after Koch's discovery, the great French chemist Louis Pasteur developed a vaccine, the first ever produced, to treat anthrax. He quickly followed it up with another vaccine to treat rabies, a disease that was very common in Europe at the time. Paul Ehrlich, who worked in Koch's laboratory, produced a dramatically effective drug, which he called a "magic bullet," to treat syphilis. The combined efforts of Koch, Pasteur, and Ehrlich led to treatments for tuberculosis, diphtheria, typhoid fever, and cholera. The knowledge they gained and the techniques they developed transformed the field of medicine from a confused, superstitious muddle into a highly efficient discipline for fighting and controlling infectious diseases.

But knowing how to identify bacteria and how to control them when they become infectious is a long way from being able to repair a damaged spinal cord or to cure cancer or Alzheimer's disease. Curing such diseases requires a deep knowledge of the cell's genes, molecules, and metabolic pathways. But in those days most questions regarding basic cell biology drew a complete blank. Not until the 1930s did histochemists and biochemists begin unraveling some of the details of cellular behavior, but still they knew nothing about the gene's coding for the cellular structures and functions that were being discovered. They could not even agree on which type of molecule, DNA, or protein was the genetic material. Many scientists believed such questions could never be answered and that our knowledge of the cell would always remain superficial. By 1940 the euphoria of the late 1800s had given way to disappointment and confusion.

The outlook began to brighten in 1952, when Martha Chase and Alfred Hershey proved that DNA, and not protein, is the genetic material of a cell. Their experiment depended on the fact that bacteria, like people, are subject to viral infections. A virus that infects a bacterium is called bacteriophage, or phage for short. Using the newly developed electron microscopes, other scientists had been able to observe a phage attaching to a bacterial cell, after which the virus, acting like a tiny syringe, injected a long molecule into the bacterium. Within a few hours, phage particles could be seen forming inside the bacteria, after which the cell lysed, or burst open, releasing the newly made daughter phage to infect other bacteria. What did the parental phage inject into the bacteria: protein, DNA, or both? This is the question everyone wanted to answer. In a beautifully elegant experiment, Chase and Hershey showed that the phage always injects DNA into the bacterium, not protein.

With the identity of the cell's genetic material firmly established, many scientists turned their attention to learning more about DNA,

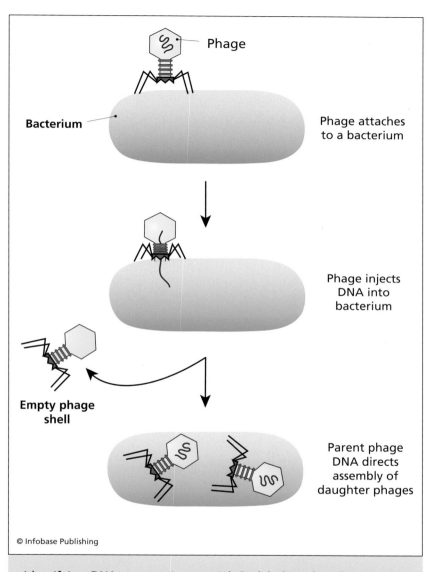

Identifying DNA as genetic material. By labeling the phages' DNA with an isotope of phosphorus and its protein with an isotope of sulfur, Martha Chase and Alfred Hershey were able to show that the phage always injects DNA into the host bacterium.

and in 1953 James Watson and Francis Crick published a model for the structure of this macromolecule. DNA was shown to be a double helix, consisting of a linear sequence of four different nucleotides encoding the genetic information. In their paper, published in 1953 in the journal *Nature* and entitled *A Structure for Deoxyribose Nucleic Acid,* Watson and Crick pointed out that the process of complementary nucleotide pairing provides a simple mechanism for gene duplication prior to cell division. Within 10 years, other scientists worked out the complete genetic code used by all living cells.

Understanding the molecular nature of the gene reinvigorated the biology community, giving biologists renewed hope that they could answer some of the following questions: How many genes does a cell have and how are they controlled? Which genes are necessary for the day-to-day running of the cell (now called housekeeping genes) and which are needed for embryonic development? Is there a gene for intelligence as there are genes for eye and hair color? Do cells become cancerous because a gene is not functioning properly, and if so, which one is responsible? Is Alzheimer's disease produced by a defective gene? The questions are endless, and despite the renewed enthusiasm, most biologists realized that it would take a new technology to provide the answers, a technology capable of isolating and amplifying specific genes so their sequence could be determined and their behavior studied in detail.

Throughout the 1960s there was no way to study a gene in detail. DNA encoded the genes in a sequence of nucleotides, but there was no way to determine the exact sequence, nor was it possible to study a gene's activity or expression profile; that is, when it is turned on or off. This began to change in the 1970s with the isolation and purification of protein enzymes that could cut DNA at specific sites and other enzymes that could join two DNA fragments together. These enzymes led the way to the development of recombinant DNA technology, or biotechnology, which made it possible for scientists to study genes and their many functions in great detail.

Since the 1970s scientists around the world have used biotechnology to gain a deep understanding of cellular structure and function. The cell cycle, observed by microbiologists since the late 1800s, was finally described in exquisite detail as the molecular components were identified and their genes isolated and sequenced. This information was crucial to the success of Ian Wilmut's cloning experiments.

Cancer researchers also relied heavily on this information as they struggled to gain an understanding of how the cell cycle changed when a cell became cancerous. Neuroscientists, desperate in their attempts to stop the mental devastation caused by Alzheimer's disease, finally were able to understand the reason for the neuronal death that always accompanies this disease. Embryologists, hard at work since the days of Hans Spemann, identified many of the genes responsible for the seemingly miraculous conversion of an egg cell into a multicellular organism. Scientists observing this transformation realized that the most important talent a cell has is its ability to communicate with other cells and the world around it. The cell's communication hardware, known as the glycocalyx, was identified and studied in great detail, giving birth to a new branch of biology known as signal transduction.

The insights gained from the study of signal transduction proved invaluable when scientists began studying stem cells. These cells were discovered in the 1950s by Drs. Ernest McCulloch and James Till, currently emeritus professors at the University of Toronto. Stem cells were isolated from human embryos in 1998 by Dr. James Thomson at the University of Wisconsin and from adult tissues in 2001 by Dr. Catherine Verfaille at the University of Minnesota.

HUMAN CLONES

Cloning a patient is the first and crucial step in therapeutic cloning: Without the cloned embryo there is no therapy. But the ability to clone a human has so far evaded all attempts, even though the basic procedure was described more than 10 years ago when Dolly

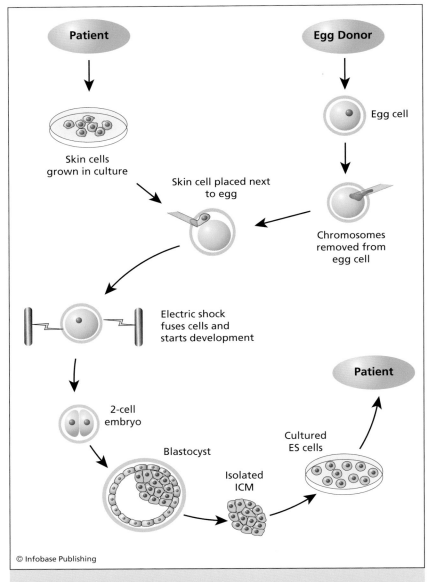

Patient

Egg Donor

Egg cell

Skin cells
grown in culture

Skin cell placed next
to egg

Chromosomes
removed from
egg cell

Electric shock
fuses cells and
starts development

Patient

2-cell
embryo

Blastocyst

Cultured
ES cells

Isolated
ICM

© Infobase Publishing

Therapeutic cloning. This procedure involves cloning a patient in order to obtain ES cells. Once the embryo develops to the blastocyst stage, the ICM is isolated, and the resulting ES cells are grown in culture before being used to treat that same patient.

the sheep was cloned. Part of the reason for this is due to the extremely low efficiency of somatic cell nuclear transfer, with only one out of 277 sheep embryos going to term. Cloning efficiency of farm animals has improved over the years but is still less than 1 percent. There are bound to be some slight differences between farm animals and humans with regard to this procedure, which could easily mark the difference between success and failure.

Another reason for the difficulty of obtaining human clones is almost certainly due to the ethical controversy that has limited funding for this kind of research and the availability of human oocytes. In the United States, researchers cannot by law offer to pay women for their eggs although they can accept donations. Nevertheless, for nearly eight years researchers in Europe and the United States tried but failed to obtain cloned human embryos. It was thus a shock to the research community when, in 2004, scientists at Seoul National University (SNU) in South Korea, announced that they had succeeded in cloning human embryos and had produced patient-specific ES cells. Korean scientists and politicians were still celebrating the accomplishment when an investigation at SNU concluded that the work was fraudulent: Stem cell enthusiasts were still without a protocol.

HUMAN-ANIMAL HYBRIDS

Many scientists believe the difficulty in producing patient-specific ES cells is due to the shortage of human oocytes; that this shortage, even more than the ethical controversy, has slowed the pace of research so much that it could take another decade before the problem is solved. As an alternative, researchers in the United Kingdom have suggested using cow or pig eggs. That is, instead of transferring the human nucleus into an enucleated human egg, transfer it into an enucleated cow's egg. After a few days of development, human ES cells could be isolated from the hybrid embryo. Scientists in the United Kingdom produced the first human-cow hybrid embryos in

April 2008 but have yet to isolate usable ES cells. If they do, it will make therapeutic cloning a practical reality.

But there are many problems associated with human-animal hybrids. Society in general is appalled at the idea of creating such hybrids and believes it is profoundly unethical. From the therapeutic standpoint, there are dangers enough when it comes to introducing normal ES cells into a patient, let alone cross-species hybrid cells. While it is true that the cow's nucleus is removed and that development is guided by the human genome, the full story is not so straightforward. The earliest stages of embryonic development are controlled by factors supplied by the egg and not by the nucleus. Thus for the first few hours of development cow factors are in charge and are bound to leave an imprint of some kind. This imprint could affect the immunological compatibility of the ES cells when used to treat a patient.

In addition, mitochondria are inherited through the maternal line. That is, the embryo does not make them but gets them from the egg. Mitochondria are extremely important organelles that provide the cell with energy. If a hybrid embryo were allowed to grow into an adult, that individual would look human, but every cell in his or her body would be powered by cow mitochondria. All mitochondria, regardless of their source, have their own genome, so they are able to make some of their own enzymes, but they depend on the cell nucleus for several important factors. Whether the human nucleus can provide the cow mitochondria with the necessary factors is still to be determined. How these potential incompatibilities will affect the viability of the hybrid ES cells is anyone's guess.

As stated above, "A transgenic sheep or goat looks like any other sheep or goat, and the transgenes they carry, rather than turning them into monsters, will help save the lives of millions of people worldwide." This is true, but only for those clones designed to produce therapeutic biomolecules. Since 2005 a new kind of transgenic animal has been produced by scientists studying neurological disorders, such as Parkinson's disease (PD). In this case, human embryonic neural stem cells have been introduced into mouse embryos, resulting in human-mouse hybrids that look like mice, but nearly 1 percent of their brains are constructed from human neurons (differentiated from the stem cells). Whether the stem cell-derived neurons construct humanlike circuitry is yet to be determined, but before such work could be approved for treating PD, it would have to be repeated using primates, where the percentage of human stem cells forming the brain is expected to be much higher than it is in the more distantly related mouse. As a consequence, the outcome of these experiments could be a monkey or a chimpanzee that has a humanized brain. In such a case, Dr. Moreau's beast-people may not be so far-fetched after all.

FUTURE PROSPECTS

The future of therapeutic cloning is uncertain. Aside from the ethical problems associated with human embryonic stem cell research and the production of human-animal hybrids, no one to date has been able to produce patient-specific ES cells with this procedure. Moreover, Japanese scientists have recently produced a new kind of stem cell called an induced pluripotent stem (iPS) cell that is likely to make therapeutic cloning obsolete. These cells are produced by reprogramming skin cells to something that is equivalent to ES cells. IPS cells are patient-specific, relatively easy to produce, and do not require human eggs or the killing of human embryos. This procedure has been refined to the point that it is now possible to reprogram a skin cell directly into another type of cell, such as a neuron, thus bypassing the ES cell stage altogether. Some scientists still believe therapeutic cloning has merit, but Ian Wilmut, inventor of the core technology, is not among them. Dr. Wilmut recently announced that he was giving up on this procedure in favor of iPS cells and is currently in charge of a cellular reprogramming group at the University of Edinburgh.

7

Ethical Issues

U ntil the late 1990s, the idea of animal cloning wafted around a few research laboratories as an abstract concept that was fun to ponder but not to be taken seriously. Dolly changed all that. Since the day she was born, scientists, politicians, philosophers, and the general public have been debating the ethical consequences of animal cloning. Dolly converted what was once an idle topic of conversation into something that could affect us all, a new technology that could rejuvenate our medical science and revolutionize animal husbandry.

Scientists like to think they have a solid grip on this technology and are comfortable with its future prospects. But when something looks too good to be true, it is wise to step back and ask the simple question: What will cost us? Not in dollars and cents, but in the ideas and beliefs that have shaped our culture and ourselves—ideas and beliefs that have taken thousands of years to develop and now stand at

the core of our legal and moral systems. Yes, animal cloning will revolutionize animal husbandry, but it will also change forever the way
humankind thinks about its families, its children, and one another.

These assessments may seem overstated; after all, identical twins
are clones of each other, and there seems to be no great problem
there. But twinning is a natural event and, more important, one
that brings life, not one that takes life away. Animal cloning, on
the other hand, is already being used to create human embryos for
therapeutic cloning. Cloning is also being used to produce highly
controversial experimental organisms that are human-animal hybrids. The ethical consequences of cloning are, by necessity, intri-
cately linked to a much broader issue that deals with the basic care
of farm and research animals.

FARM ANIMALS

Animal rights groups have long complained about the living conditions of farm animals, many of which are confined in cramped quar-
ters without enough room for proper exercise, let alone a normal
quality of life. Although there are humane societies that attempt to
protect them from outright cruelty and abuse, farm animals, except
for horses, have no legal rights. The recent controversy in California,
regarding the rearing of laying hens is a case in point. These animals
are kept in cages so small that they cannot stand up or turn around.
Californians for Humane Farms, sponsored by the Humane Society of the United States and other animal welfare groups submitted
ballot proposition 2 (the Prevention of Farm Animal Cruelty Act)
to the California secretary of state for consideration in that state's
general election of November 4, 2008. Proposition 2 called specifically for an increase in the size of the cages laying hens were being
kept in. This proposition was passed by the public with 63 percent of
the votes in favor and will take effect in 2015. Although this law will
force the farmers to increase the size of each cage, the fact is that
these animals, otherwise known as battery hens, will sit in small
cages for their entire lives and never see the light of day.

Given this situation, what could cloning do to make these animals worse off than they are already? The ethical dilemma of cloning farm animals falls under the category of cruelty and abuse. This is not to say that cloning a farm animal is cruel and abusive but simply that the potential is there. The current efficiency of animal cloning is extremely low. This means that in addition to many stillbirths and naturally aborted fetuses, there are many live births of abnormal offspring that will be afflicted with a higher proportion of diseases and disabilities than would a naturally conceived animal. Given that the risks are known—having seen, for example, cloned animals struggle because of an early onset of arthritis or lung disease brought on by a defective immune system—is it right to go on cloning these creatures? Animal rights groups would answer with an emphatic no. Scientists answer this question with a qualified no: No, it is not right to clone animals if they will suffer unduly, but if the cloning-related disease is mild or controllable, then for the sake of discovery, the experiments should continue. Moreover, what looks like an unethical procedure now may only be an artifact of cloning's current state of development. Perhaps 10 years from now, after the technology improves, cloned animals will be as healthy as naturally conceived animals, and therefore the ethical dilemma will disappear. They will become, in effect, just another farm animal, no better off, but no worse off, either.

RESEARCH ANIMALS

The overall dilemma of cloning research on animals is very similar to that described for farm animals. But research animals deserve a separate discussion because there are some important differences. Farm animals are kept for food, while research animals are kept to further our knowledge of biology, most of which is used to develop new medical technologies that often save many thousands of lives.

The question of cruelty and abuse still exists, but now the ethical issues are more complex. Is it wrong to clone a research animal that may suffer physically as a consequence of being cloned if that suffering will, somewhere down the road, relieve the suffering of thousands, possibly millions, of people? The answer to this question varies considerably depending on whether it comes from animal rights groups, scientists, or government regulatory agencies. Animal rights groups have stated emphatically that it is wrong to experiment on warm-blooded animals regardless of the potential benefits. Government agencies want to encourage research, but at the same time have called for a more responsible attitude toward the care and maintenance of research animals, and in particular, more stringent regulations to ensure that the animals do not suffer unduly. Scientists, of course, believe that animal cloning should be allowed, and like ranchers raising beef cattle, want to regulate the business themselves without external pressures or interference. An early attempt to deal with this issue came with the Animal Welfare Acts, passed in the United States in 1966 and in the United Kingdom in 2006. These acts required that every animal facility has an attending veterinarian who must ensure that adequate veterinary care is provided at all times. In practice, this meant that each facility had to establish a special committee, called an Institutional Animal Care and Use Committee, to monitor the use of research animals and to ensure that their treatment is humane. Researchers must inform these committees of their intent and justify the use of an animal, particularly if the animal will suffer as a consequence of the research. The veterinarian and the committee members must then decide whether the merits of the experiment justify the expected suffering of the animal. In 2002 the U.S. government stripped its own Animal Welfare Act (AWA) of much of its effectiveness by taking birds, rats, and mice out of the definition of "animal." It has been estimated that U.S. researchers use more than 100 million mice each year, and thus these animals represent the most common type of research animal by far. Because of the amendment, federal law protects none of these animals, and consequently researchers may use them as they wish. Dr. Larry Carbone, a veterinarian who has studied the plight of research animals, has described scientists who use and dispose of laboratory mice as though they were pieces of tissue paper.

The plight of research animals that are still protected by the AWA, such as monkeys, rabbits, dogs, and cats, is not much better. The decision to allow an invasive experiment on any of these animals is fairly straightforward, and such experiments are rarely rejected. Thousands of research centers routinely subject these animals to painful experiments in which they are crippled surgically or deliberately infected with a debilitating and usually fatal disease. Placing the treatment and care of these animals (and those that are no longer classified as animals) in the hands of scientists who depend on them for data is no better than allowing wolves to guard the sheep. The convenient declassification of the ubiquitous lab mouse is a case in point.

The situation is even worse for invertebrates. The AWA does not cover cold-blooded animals, and thus there are no guidelines or welfare committees for insects. Researchers using locusts, houseflies, cockroaches, and any number of other insect species may do what they like with them. A famous English insect physiologist, Vincent B. Wigglesworth, made stunning discoveries by cutting the abdomen off one bug and attaching it with bee's wax to the abdomen of another insect. Many studies involving insect endocrinology entail cutting the head off an adult locust, sealing the wound with wax, and then, by injecting nutrients into the abdomen, keeping the animal alive in that state for several weeks.

The decision to allow an experiment to proceed becomes much more difficult when animals closely related to humans, such as monkeys, baboons, and chimpanzees, are used. No one would subject these animals to the kinds of experiments that rats, mice, and insects routinely undergo, although the living conditions of research chimpanzees is not much better than it is for battery hens. Chimpanzees

Immature desert locust *(Shistocerca gregaria)* feeding on young cereal leaves *(Nigel Cattlin/Visuals Unlimited)*

used for AIDS and hepatitis research, for example, are kept in small cages, in windowless rooms, with no access to an exercise or social area, sometimes for up to 30 years. The AWA will allow scientists to experiment on these animals, but only if they are important experiments and do not cause extreme suffering. But given the appalling living conditions, these animals suffer nevertheless.

The plight of research chimpanzees has been brought to the public's attention by animal welfare groups, such as the Jane Goodall Institute, founded in California by Dr. Goodall in 1977, and the Chimpanzee Sanctuary Northwest, founded in Washington State by Keith LaChappelle in 2002. This sanctuary has rescued many research chimpanzees by giving them a pleasant place to live where they have access to an outdoor area and where they can socialize with other chimps.

The revulsion that many people experience when confronted with the realities of animal experimentation is magnified when it comes to the question of human experimentation. Society does

Rhesus monkey in Lopburi provincial capital, Thailand *(Rob Schumann/Shutterstock, Inc.)*

condone human experimentation, but only if it is done according to rigorous guidelines. Experiments using human subjects are called clinical trials, and they form an essential part of modern-day medical research. Indeed, medical procedures are not approved for general use until they are tested in one or more clinical trials. Society accepts clinical trials because they are conducted with the full informed consent of the human experimental subjects. The concept of informed consent has led to a heated debate when it comes to the idea of cloning humans, as discussed in a following section.

HUMAN CLONES

Practically from the day that Dolly was born, speculation about the cloning of humans began to grow. The initial enthusiasm for cloning humans may have been caused by the sheer novelty of the idea, since there were few in the scientific community or the general public who could offer sound reasons for attempting such a thing. Vague notions about immortality and the ability to replace extra-bright people gave way to more practical motivations, such as replacing a loved one or making it possible for sterile or same-sex couples to have children. Scientists involved in the cloning of Dolly and in particular, Ian Wilmut, the team leader, made it clear very early on that cloning is not an avenue to immortality. A person's clone would be an identical twin, not a replacement. The two would look alike, talk alike, and maybe even dress alike. But they would be distinct individuals, with their own memories and separate identities. The idea of using cloning to replace gifted individuals naturally raises the question of just what constitutes a gifted individual and who will get to decide what those characteristics are. Is winning a prize, such as a Noble Prize, a reliable benchmark for cloning eligibility? People who work in blue-collar jobs, or perhaps do not work at all, are just as likely to have the human qualities that everyone should strive for. This is a profound ethical dilemma. It presupposes that humans have the wisdom to know which kind of person will improve our societies and make the world a better place for us all. Yet who can claim such wisdom? And therefore, who can claim that cloning, for the purpose of enhancing the human race, is a good idea?

If it is unwise to clone people to improve the human race, does it follow that it is also unwise to allow sterile or same sex couples to use cloning so that they can have children? Theoretically, there is nothing wrong with couples wanting to clone themselves as a way to start a family; various invertebrate species have been doing so, with great success, for a very long time. However, at the present time, it is an unethical choice to make. Cloning, as made clear by the Dolly experiment, is very inefficient. Most animal clone embryos die before reaching full term, while many others die in the course of being born. Those clones that make it to adulthood are likely to carry subtle genetic abnormalities that weaken their immune system and make them susceptible to obesity and arthritis. Should we clone our children and subject them to such risks? Probably not, given that sterile couples today have the option of starting a family by using standard in vitro fertilization techniques or by adopting a child.

As an ethical dilemma cloning for reproduction is a difficult, but not insurmountable problem. Ethical objections, particularly concerning therapeutic cloning, fall under the category of human experimentation and are discussed with great clarity in the Belmont Report, produced in 1976 by the U.S. Department of Health (see chapter 10 for details). This report established three basic ethical principles that apply any procedure that involves humans: respect for persons, beneficence, and informed consent.

Respect for persons in the context of clinical trials demands that subjects enter into research voluntarily and with adequate information. This assumes the individuals are autonomous agents, that is, are competent to make up their own minds. However, there are many instances where potential research subjects are not really autonomous: prisoners, patients in a mental institution, children, the elderly and the infirm. Many would argue that human embryos and fetuses should also fall within this category. All of these people require special protection to ensure they are not being coerced or fooled into volunteering as research subjects. Beneficence is generally regarded as acts of kindness or charity, but in a research context it is an obligation. It is not enough to respect a potential subject's decisions and to protect them from harm, but in addition, it is necessary to do all that is possible to ensure their well-being. All participants in clinical trials must provide informed consent, in writing. Moreover, steps must be taken to ensure the consent is in fact informed. This might involve an independent assessment of the individual's ability to understand the language on the consent form, and any instructions or explanations the investigators have given.

The Belmont report coincides with a growing consensus in the world that human cloning is an unethical form of human experimentation and should not be done. Consequently, legislators around the world have already taken steps to regulate the practice or ban it altogether. But a confluence of technologies, culminating in therapeutic cloning, has made cloning the center of a debate that is not specifically addressed by the Belmont Report and may be extremely difficult to resolve.

Anti-abortion groups, the Catholic church, and many people in the general public are strongly opposed to the idea of using human embryos as research subjects and, in particular, are opposed to the idea of creating human life as a disposable source of ES cells. Their objection is based on many of the principles described in the Belmont Report. Society takes offense at research that uses animals closely related to humans, and quite naturally, that offense rises to a maximum when it involves research on human patients. Society allows research on humans, but only because of the policy of informed consent. Embryos cannot give informed consent, but it is safe to assume that if they could, they would choose life over death. In the case of abortion, ethicists and legislators have deferred to the rights of the woman over the rights of the embryo or the fetus. But in the case of therapeutic cloning, there is no such deferral possible, and therefore, within the context of the Belmont Report, there can be no ethical grounds for the production of human embryos as a source of stem cells.

Proponents of therapeutic cloning claim that the medical therapies that could be derived from embryonic stem cells override the ethical problems. However, the Belmont Report, while not specifically addressing the issue of therapeutic cloning, is broad enough to cover ethical issues. Society may agree that giving mice a lethal case of cancer is acceptable if there is a chance it may lead to a cure for humans, but choosing to sacrifice human embryos in order to save other human lives contravenes the intent of the ethical principles established by the report. Some advocates of therapeutic cloning suggest that because the embryos are cloned, they are not really human, and therefore an ethical dilemma does not exist. But other scientists reject the premise that clones are inherently less than, or even different from, their conventionally conceived genetic counterparts. In particular, when Dolly was cloned, Ian Wilmut and many other scientists went to great lengths to assure everyone that Dolly was a normal sheep in every way, and that being a clone did not change that. Dolly even went on to bear, by natural means, several healthy lambs and, aside from having her picture published on the cover of *Time* magazine, led a very ordinary life. Consequently, a cloned human embryo deserves the same ethical and legal protection as does a human embryo conceived by natural means.

Advocates of therapeutic cloning, in their eagerness to exploit the properties of embryonic stem cells, have overlooked the great potential of adult stem cells (i.e., stem cells isolated from the bone marrow of adults or from umbilical cord blood) and iPS cells. The research of Catherine Verfaille has shown that these cells also possess developmental plasticity and, in the case of bone marrow stem cells, can be harvested from the patients needing treatment, thus eliminating both potential immune rejection and the ethical problems associated with the use of embryos. Medical therapies based on AS or iPS cells can be developed faster than therapies requiring embryonic stem cells and will be free of the ethical problems associated with therapeutic cloning.

Curing diseases that affect us now, like Alzheimer's or cancer, requires very powerful technologies that probe deep into our cells. Before we consent to using them, however, we must consider whether these techniques compromise what many regard as the essence of our humanity. If we jump for the quick fix, without reflecting on what we believe is right and wrong, we may end up like an old Greek statue: nice to look at and impervious to disease, but cold as stone.

HUMAN-ANIMAL HYBRIDS

The first human-animal hybrid was produced in 2006, when scientists injected human stem cells into the developing brains of mouse embryos. By the time the mice reached adulthood, it was estimated that their brains consisted of nearly a million human-derived brain cells, which amounts to about 0.1 percent of a mouse's brain. It is not yet clear whether the human-derived neurons organized themselves into a humanlike circuit or whether they produced a viable mouse circuit.

Scientists conduct experiments like these in the hope of learning more about human neurological disorders. But the effects that such an experiment may have on the animal are clearly difficult to estimate. It has been suggested that animals like these be carefully monitored for signs of humanized behavior, but no one knows what "humanized behavior" is going to look like, and given the declassification of mice by the AWA, it is unlikely that scientists will take the initiative in this regard.

In 2008 U.K. scientists produced another kind of human-animal hybrid. In this case, the hybrid is produced with the nuclear transfer procedure used to clone Dolly, but instead of using a human egg, the nucleus is transferred into an enucleated cow's egg. Critics insist that this procedure is unethical and immoral by any standard. Scientists, instead of offering an intelligent rebuttal, have simply stated that the potential of this procedure is so great that it outweighs the ethical considerations. In this instance, scientists appear to have taken the Cole Porter song "Anything Goes" to heart. This attitude, more than anything else, highlights the danger of allowing a special-interest, highly focused group (the scientists) to sway public policy. When it comes to research, scientists follow the nose, and they usually do so without reference to an overarching moral scheme. If a human-cow hybrid can solve the problem of human egg shortage, then it must be a good thing. The British government, apparently impressed with this argument, has given its approval, but legal challenges are pending.

In any case, it is unlikely that these hybrid embryos will ever prove effective. Indeed, Dr. Robert Lanza and his team have recently shown that human-animal hybrid embryos are generally defective and display an abnormal gene expression profile. In particular, these hybrids fail to express critical pluripotency-associated genes, thus rendering them unusable as a source of patient-specific stem cells.

8

Legal Issues

Dolly's birth and the perfection of nuclear transfer technology provided powerful new methods for the production of transgenic animals and for medical therapies. They also introduced many ethical problems that forced governments in Europe and North America to introduce legislation designed to control the use and spread of this technology. The legal issues are focused on two forms of human cloning. The first is reproductive cloning, whereby an embryo is produced by nuclear transfer and then carried to term by a surrogate mother, as was done with Dolly. The second form is known as therapeutic cloning, whereby an embryo is cloned solely for the purpose of harvesting the inner cell mass, or ES cells, for use in a variety of medical therapies. Thus this form of cloning involves stem cell therapy and has proven to be the most difficult issue to resolve. The legal debate varies from country to country, particularly for therapeutic cloning. The discussion begins by considering the legal issues as they unfolded in the United Kingdom (England, Wales, Scotland, and Northern Ireland), for it was there that laws regulating human cloning were first discussed and enacted.

THE UNITED KINGDOM

The regulation of human cloning in the United Kingdom is governed by the Human Fertilization and Embryology Act of 1990. This legislation, administered by the Human Fertilization and Embryology Authority (HFEA), was enacted to regulate the practice of in vitro fertilization (IVF), which originated in Britain with the birth of the first "test tube" baby, Louise Brown, in 1973. HFEA was established after a great deal of discussion, both inside and outside the British Parliament, which was stimulated by the Committee of Inquiry into Human Fertilization and Embryology. This committee was chaired by Baroness Warnock and was tabled in 1984. The Act of 1990, however, largely implemented the recommendations of the Warnock committee.

Under the act, research on embryos older than 14 days is prohibited. This time period was set to coincide with the appearance of the primitive streak, an anatomical feature of an embryo that indicates the beginning of neurulation and the formation of the central nervous system. All research dealing with human embryos is licensed by the HFEA, which may be denied if the authority feels the research objectives may be obtained with nonhuman embryos or by some other means. In general, the license is granted if the research is focused on treatments for infertility, development of contraceptives, or if the results are expected to clarify the causes of miscarriages.

With the birth of Dolly, the HFEA and the Human Genetics Advisory Commission undertook a public consultation on human cloning. Their report, entitled *Cloning Issues in Reproduction, Science and Medicine* was tabled in 1998. The report recommended that the HFEA issue licenses for therapeutic cloning and that re-

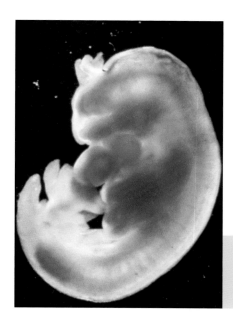

Human embryo, two to three weeks old *(Claude Edelmann/ Photo Researchers, Inc.)*

search involving the embryos so produced would be subject to the 14-day limit imposed by the act for normally, or IVF, conceived embryos. These recommendations were debated at length by the British government and passed into law as the Human Fertilization and Embryology Regulations (HFER) on January 22, 2001. The passage of this law brought with it the concern that some of the cloned embryos might be implanted into a surrogate mother and brought to full term. To ensure that this did not happen, the government introduced the Human Reproductive Cloning bill, which proposed a ban on reproductive cloning. This bill was passed into law on December 4, 2001, and is still in effect.

The British legislation regulating therapeutic cloning (HFER 2001) was reviewed by a special committee set up by the House of Lords in 2002. This committee put out a call for evidence from the scientific and research organizations, the churches, medical charities, patients' support groups, pro-life groups, and many organizations representing the general public, such as the trades unions, and the National Federation of Women's Institutes. The committee received 52 submissions from various organizations, and they held 12 sessions of oral evidence at which 42 people representing 17 organizations presented their arguments for or against the proposed legislation. Members of the committee also visited research laboratories to gain a better understanding of the science involved. While confirming majority support for HFER 2001, the committee's report called for increased surveillance of therapeutic cloning projects to ensure that every cloned embryo is accounted for, and that the experiments to which the embryos are subjected do not extend beyond what is allowed by law.

Critics believe the British government and the HFEA are simply bowing to pressure from science lobbyists. Moreover, they have argued that the 14-day limit is nothing more than a boundary of convenience since the legislators know that scientists want embryos that are less than a week old. Consequently, the attempt to define a point at which a human embryo can or cannot be destroyed is in itself unethical. Despite public criticism, HFER's licensing decisions have become increasingly controversial:

- ▶ In 2004 they began granting British scientists a license to produce cloned human cells, making it only the second country in the world to permit such a procedure (South Korea was the first). This is essentially a license to perform therapeutic cloning.

- ▶ In 2006 they approved the screening of embryos for genes that may lead to certain cancers in middle age. Such a test will encourage abortions even though the function of these genes is poorly understood.

- ▶ In 2007 the Authority gave women permission to donate their eggs to research projects, provided strong safeguards are put in place to ensure the women are properly informed of the risks of the procedure and are protected from coercion. Critics have argued that the amount they are offering (£250 or about $460) is an inducement that many poor women will be unable to resist and many others are likely to be coerced. The Authority insists that the women will be interviewed to ensure the donation is for altruistic reasons and not for monetary gain, but it will be impossible to know this for sure. In addition, there is a low but well-recognized risk of developing ovarian hyperstimulation syndrome, which can occur during the extraction of eggs. This syndrome can damage a woman's fertility and even cause death.

► In January 2008, over the objection of a large proportion of the public, the HFEA granted licenses to Newcastle University and King's College London to carry out cytoplasmic hybrid research projects. These projects involve the production of human-animal hybrids, either by fusing human and animal cells or by transplanting human cells into animal embryos and allowing those animals to reach adulthood. This procedure could lead to the birth of a mouse, for example, that has a humanized brain.

THE EUROPEAN UNION

The European Union (EU), which includes Germany, France, Spain, the Netherlands, and 23 other European countries, agrees with the U.K. position on reproductive cloning and has passed laws to ban it. However, the EU strongly disagrees with the U.K. on the issue of therapeutic cloning. Article 18 of the Council of European Convention on Human Rights and Biomedicine states categorically that "the creation of human embryos for research purposes is prohibited." Thus therapeutic cloning, or any kind of research that destroys human embryos, is illegal in Germany, Italy, Austria, Finland,

France, Portugal, Ireland, the Netherlands, and Poland. In addition, the Council of Europe, which now has 47 member states, including Russia and Turkey, adopted a convention on biomedicine that prohibits the creation of human embryos for research purposes. Liberal European countries, such as France and the Netherlands, appeared willing to allow therapeutic cloning and provided laws that were enacted to prohibit placing such embryos in surrogate mothers to be carried to full term. But it became clear that enforcing such a law would be nearly impossible, and so a complete ban on all forms of cloning seemed to be the only practical solution.

In spring 2008 the German parliament voted to amend its stem cell law, which had restricted scientists to working on cell lines created before January 1, 2002. The amendment advances the cut-off date to May 1, 2007. It will also no longer be a criminal offense for German scientists to use even newer cell lines in countries where such research is allowed. By extending the cut-off date, legislators have given researchers access to an additional 500 cell lines. Most German scientists were hoping for a complete abandonment of the cut-off date, but the legislation has been accepted as a reasonable compromise.

THE UNITED STATES

A bill to prohibit all forms of cloning (Human Cloning Prohibition Act of 2001, H.R. 2505), which had the support of President George Bush, was passed by the House of Representatives in July 2001 but has not as yet been written into law. The bill, introduced by Representatives David Weldon (R-Florida) and Bart Stupak (D-Michigan) had a broad base of support but met with opposition when submitted to the Senate for debate in 2002. Dissension came from patient advocate groups and members of the biomedical research community, who agreed to a ban on reproductive cloning but argued in favor of therapeutic cloning. However, neither side could show that they had at least 60 votes needed to bring the bill to a vote. Consequently, then Senate majority leader Tom Daschle put the gridlocked issue aside.

In 2003 the House of Representatives took a second vote on the bill, and this time it was approved by an overwhelming margin of 241 to 155. Senator Sam Brownback (R-Kansas) introduced the companion bill to the Senate for debate. Both bills call for a maximum penalty of $1 million in civil fines and up to 10-year jail terms for those who attempt reproductive or therapeutic cloning. Competing legislation was also submitted by Senators Arlen Specter (R-Pennsylvania) and Dianne Feinstein (D-California), which calls for a ban only on reproductive cloning.

Frustrated by the federal restrictions, several states held referendums to seek the public's permission to allocate state funds to establish and fund embryonic stem cell research, including therapeutic cloning. California, Connecticut, Illinois, Maryland, and New Jersey obtained voter approval between 2004 and 2005. At the federal level, Democrats in the House of Representatives introduced the Stem Cell Research Enhancement Act of 2005 (H.R. 810). After a lengthy debate, the bill was passed by the House and later by the Senate, but failed to get the two-thirds majority needed to block a presidential veto. President Bush, true to his word, vetoed the bill in July 2006. In his veto message, President Bush explained his objection to the bill in his opening paragraph: "Like all Americans, I believe our Nation must vigorously pursue the tremendous possibilities that science offers to cure disease and improve the lives of millions. Yet, as science brings us ever closer to unlocking the secrets of human biology, it also offers temptations to manipulate human life and violate human dignity. Our conscience and history as a Nation demand that we resist this temptation. With the right scientific techniques and the right policies, we can achieve scientific progress while living up to our ethical responsibilities."

In the following year, House Democrats reintroduced H.R. 810. They lobbied Republicans in both chambers of Congress in the hope of winning a two-thirds majority. Although they were successful in bringing more Republicans over to their side, the bill, although passing in both chambers, failed again to get a two-thirds majority. The bill was sent to President Bush, who vetoed it on June 20, 2007, for the second time.

Politicians and the scientific community were greatly disappointed that the bill was vetoed. Both groups were convinced that the public wanted the restrictions on ES cell research lifted. Pollsters have indeed reported public sympathy for the Democrat's bill, but polls can be misleading, particularly when dealing with a complex topic that is shrouded in hyperbole and misinformation. Surprisingly, much of the misinformation is coming from the scientists themselves, who have consistently downplayed the potential of adult stem and iPS cells while leaving the impression that research in the field cannot continue without embryonic stem cells. This view is not supported by the facts: To date, not a single clinical trial has been launched that involves ES cells compared to more than 2,000 adult stem cell trials that are currently being funded by NIH. Even if scientists had an inexhaustible supply of ES cells to work with, owing to the dangers of GVHD and teratomas, they would not be able to use them in clinical trials.

Scientists have complained that President Bush's policies hampered the progress of stem cell research. This argument was in full force when it appeared that Dr. Hwang's results were reliable. American scientists were sure he had won the race because of a difference in funding. But scientists in the United Kingdom also failed to produce patient-specific ES cells, even though they have ample funding and unrestricted access to human embryos. Consequently, it seems more likely that the pace of embryonic stem cell research in the United States has to do with the difficulty of the problem itself and not the availability of ES cell lines or research funds. U.S. researchers have also complained that without greater access to human ES cells they will never be able to identify species-specific cellular mechanisms that control pluripotency, but researchers at Harvard University have recently completed a genome-wide analysis of mouse ES cells that has identified several mechanisms that appear to be applicable to any ES cell regardless of its source.

Nevertheless, American stem cell researchers remain committed to the goal of gaining greater access to human ES cells. On March 9, 2009, they got their wish when President Barack Obama signed an executive order reversing his predecessor's restrictions on the funding of ES cell research. However, congressional restrictions still remain. Although scientists can now receive government grants to do research on new stem cell lines grown in privately funded labs, they cannot use federal financing to produce new ES cell lines. Moreover, a recent Gallup poll showed that while a slight majority of the American public (52 percent) support President Obama's decision, most Americans, regardless of political affiliation or religious sentiment, want some sort of restrictions in place. Thus it would seem that the real political and social battle over this issue has only just begun.

9

Commercialization of Animal Cloning

Producing transgenic pharmaceuticals is a difficult and risky business. The basic research is difficult, the clinical trials are difficult, and the whole developmental process, from research to approved drug, takes about 12 years and is extremely expensive. Current estimates for the cost of bringing a novel drug to market in the United States range from $800 million to $2 billion. This estimate is based on the research and development costs of 68 randomly selected new drugs obtained from a survey of 10 pharmaceutical firms. The high-end estimate may seem cheap to Pfizer, the world's largest pharmaceutical company, which is known to have spent almost $800 million for a Phase III trial to test a single drug. Even after a company spends millions of dollars to develop a drug, only one in 5,000 compounds prove to be successful.

Consequently, companies that attempt to bring new drugs to market succeed only if they are large and very wealthy. Small biotech firms are usually forced to form a partnership with large pharmaceutical companies and to sell shares in their company to raise the necessary capital. This chapter profiles four companies of modest size that are involved in the production of transgenic drugs: the Roslin Institute, PPL Therapeutics, Hematech, Inc., and GTC Biotherapeutics.

ROSLIN INSTITUTE

The Roslin Institute, located in northern Scotland and named after a local village, was established in 1993 and is the place where Ian Wilmut cloned Dolly the sheep. The institute, with a staff of more than 240 scientists and research technicians, can trace its origins back to 1919 and is one of seven research centers in the United Kingdom sponsored by the Biotechnology and Biological Sciences Research Council (BBSR). In 2008 it became affiliated with the University of Edinburgh and will be moving into a new complex in 2010.

Dolly's birth made the institute famous, but the media attention that came with it was not always welcome. The Scottish government and the institute itself was uncomfortable in the limelight and was not equipped to deal with the controversy surrounding the field of animal cloning, particularly as it pertains to human cloning. Soon after Dolly was born, the government withdrew its financial support for the cloning efforts, forcing the institute to seek funding elsewhere.

In 2003 the institute was one of the first to receive a license from the Human Fertilization and Embryology Authority (HFEA) to produce human ES cells from donated embryos. The institute also tried, but failed, to produce ES cells from cloned embryos for therapeutic cloning. This work is ongoing, but as mentioned above, Ian Wilmut, the principal investigator, has abandoned ES cells in favor of iPS cells.

Currently, the institute is focused on animal health and disease control, animal breeding, biotechnology, and animal stem cell research. It also maintains a strong transgenics research program, which is now focused on chickens rather than on sheep or goats. Dr. Helen Sang has developed a line of transgenic chickens that are being used to produce an anticancer monoclonal antibody (MiR24) and human interferon, a natural antiviral compound. These compounds are produced in the oviduct of laying hens and are isolated from the eggs. Dr. Sang has shown that it is possible to obtain as much as a half-pound of MiR24 per gallon of egg white (50 g per liter).

PPL THERAPEUTICS

Located in northern Scotland, PPL Therapeutics was formed in 1993 primarily to partner with the Roslin Institute in its quest to produce animal clones. The collaboration between PPL and Roslin was extensive throughout the period leading up to the birth of Dolly. In 1998 the company produced transgenic sheep carrying the gene for human serum albumin and transgenic goats carrying the gene for antithrombin.

In 2000 the company became interested in xenotransplantation, or cross-species transplantation, where, for example, a pig's heart or kidney is transplanted into a human. The chronic shortage of human organs, especially hearts and kidneys, is the motivation behind the development of cross-species transplantation. Unfortunately, xeno-transplants are extremely dangerous because they invariably lead to a hyperacute rejection episode that is often fatal. This happened, for example, in the "Baby Fae" case in 1984, in which a baby died after receiving a baboon heart. Scientists studying organ transplantation have shown that baboon and pig cells have a glycoprotein embedded in their cell membranes that is not found in human cells. This glycoprotein, known as α-1,3-galactosyl, or alpha-gal, is synthesized by the enzyme α-1,3-galactosyl transferase, which attaches the sugar molecule to a membrane protein as though it were decorating a tree. This enzyme and others like it produce glycoproteins for the glycocalyx, a molecular forest that covers the surface of every cell, much like forests cover (or covered) the surface of the Earth. The rejection episode begins when the human immune system detects the foreign alpha-gal on the transplanted pig organ.

In 2002 PPL and one other biotech company produced transgenic pigs that had an inactivated gene for α-1,3-galactosyl transferase. Hopes ran high that such pigs would make xenotransplantation a routine medical therapy. Without the enzyme, the pig organs might be compatible with the human immune system, or at least no more incompatible than an allograft. But to date, this exciting possibility has yet to be tested in a clinical trial. PPL and other companies involved in this type of research encountered massive resistance from the public and from many scientists. The overriding fear was that pig organs could carry potentially deadly viruses that would infect the transplant patients and then spread throughout the population. The deadly AIDS virus is an example of how this can happen: Once it jumped from monkey to human, it spread quickly among humans all over the world.

As a consequence, PPL was unable to develop this line of research. Indeed, it was unable to bring any of its transgenic products to market, largely because of the expense of getting such products through a full battery of clinical trials. In 2003, after suffering losses exceeding $24 million, the company went out of business. To date, no attempt has been made to restart this company.

HEMATECH, INC.

Hematech was a small biotechnology company in Westport, Connecticut, when, in 2002 it created four transgenic calves that produced human antibodies known as immunoglobulin or gamma globulin. On February 10, 2005, the company reported the successful purification of human immunoglobulin free of viral and bovine DNA contamination. Later that year, the company expanded its operations by moving to a new and much larger facility in Sioux

Falls, South Dakota. The transgenic cattle, known as TC Bovine, are used for the production of large quantities of polyclonal antibodies, which can be used to treat a variety of medical conditions. In 2007 researchers at Hematech produced the first prion-free transgenic calves (hence free of mad-cow disease) to ensure the safety of the immunoglobulins produced by these animals, and they expect to have human antibodies, derived from immune-deficient transgenic cows, ready for market by 2011.

Hematech prefers working with cattle (instead of goats or chickens) for several reasons: Cattle make large quantities of antibodies, which can amount to almost 2.5 pounds (1.13 kg) in the blood of a single individual; cows are relatively easy to work with, and much is known about their growth requirements and medical care; finally, transgenic technology is more advanced in cattle than in any other species.

The transgenic product is isolated from the cow's blood by plasmapheresis. In this procedure whole blood is collected, the sample is centrifuged to separate the cells from the plasma, or liquid part of the blood, after which the cells are returned to the body. The plasma is shipped to a purification facility where the bovine blood components (proteins, fats, potential bacteria, and viruses) are removed. The antibodies so produced have many applications, including treating antibiotic-resistant infections, immune deficiencies, and for biodefense.

Antibiotic-Resistant Infections

Bacteria that cause common infections often become resistant to antibiotics. The Centers for Disease Control and Prevention (CDC) estimates nearly 2 million people in the United States acquire an infection while in a hospital, resulting in 90,000 deaths. Most of the types of bacteria causing these infections are resistant to at least one of the antibiotics commonly used to treat them. In contrast to antibiotics, bacteria cannot develop resistance to polyclonal antibodies, such as those produced by Hematech.

Immune Deficiencies

Some individuals, such as those suffering from AIDS, have compromised immune systems and have difficulty fighting common infections. An immune deficiency may also occur in patients being treated for cancer or those who have received an organ transplant. Immune-deficient patients currently are the largest group of users of human polyclonal antibody therapeutics. The human antibody treatments are effective but very expensive, currently ranging from $25,000 to $50,000 per year. Large-scale transgenic operations, such as those at Hematech, may help reduce the cost of these important drugs.

Biodefense

Defense against bioterrorists is an unfortunate necessity that the U.S. government and others around the world take very seriously. In the United States, the federal government is funding the development of novel therapeutics to meet the threat of widespread exposure to possibly deadly biological agents. Hematech has programs funded by the Department of Defense (DoD) and the National Institutes of Allergy and Infectious Disease (NIAID) to develop human polyclonal antibody therapeutics for botulism toxin, anthrax, and smallpox exposure.

Other Applications

Human polyclonal antibodies could be useful for treating many other diseases including organ transplant rejection, cancer, and various autoimmune diseases, such as rheumatoid arthritis.

GTC BIOTHERAPEUTICS

GTC Biotherapeutics is a company that began operations in 1995 with the establishment of a farm and purification facility near Framingham, Massachusetts. The farm is home to about 2,000 goats, imported from New Zealand, which have been certified scrapie-free by the U.S. Department of Agriculture (USDA). GTC's lead product is antithrombin, which may become the first transgenic biopharmaceutical to be approved for routine medical use. Antithrombin is a plasma protein with anticoagulant and anti-inflammatory properties. The company's transgenic form of the drug is known as ATryn.

In August 2006 the European Medicines Evaluation Agency (EMEA) approved the use of ATryn for treatment of patients with hereditary antithrombin deficiency (HD), undergoing high-risk surgery or childbirth. The drug has successfully completed Phase I clinical trials that showed that its effectiveness is equal to that of plasma-derived antithrombin. Seventeen patients were treated, and there were no clinically relevant complications or other thromboembolisms during the evaluation period in any of the patients.

In 2008 the company announced that it had completed enrollment in Phase II clinical trials for the treatment of patients suffering from HD. A minimum of 31 HD patients was required for this trial. Results for 14 of these patients were already obtained from the previous study that supported ATryn's approval in the European Union. The full clinical data package will include 90-day follow-up tests for antibody generation to ATryn, which is a typical regulatory requirement and was also part of the approval process successfully completed for the European Union. In 2009 GTC obtained final approval for the use of this drug in the United States.

GTC is also involved in the production of human serum albumin, alpha-1 antitrypsin, coagulation factors (VIII and IX), as well as monoclonal antibodies for cancer therapies. These products are all in the development stage.

10

Resource Center

Cloning an animal is a complex procedure that depends on an in-depth knowledge of cell biology and a variety of research techniques known as biotechnology. This chapter provides an introduction to these topics, as well as brief discussions of the human genome project, the Belmont report, the case of Jesse Gelsinger, and the nature of clinical trials.

CELL BIOLOGY

A cell is a microscopic life-form made from a variety of nature's building blocks. The smallest of these building blocks are sub-atomic particles known as quarks and leptons that form protons, neutrons, and electrons, which in turn form atoms. Scientists have identified more than 200 atoms, each of which represents a fundamental element of nature; carbon, oxygen, and nitrogen are common examples. Atoms, in their turn, can associate with one another

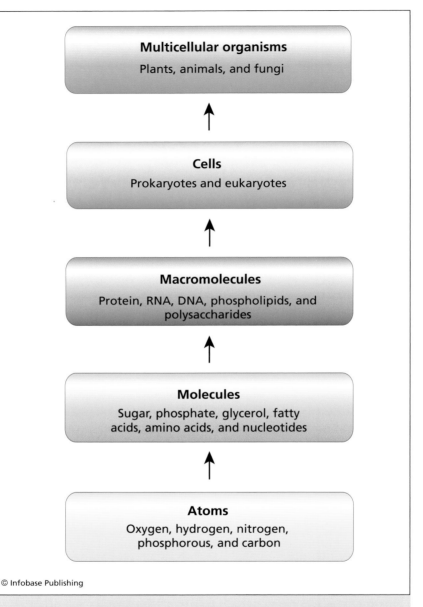

Nature's building blocks. Particles known as quarks and leptons, created in the heat of the big bang, formed the first atoms, which combined to form molecules in the oceans of the young Earth. Heat and electrical storms promoted the formation of macromolecules, providing the building blocks for cells, which in turn went on to form multicellular organisms.

to form another kind of building block known as a molecule. Sugar, for example, is a molecule constructed from carbon, oxygen, and hydrogen, while ordinary table salt is a molecule consisting of just two elements: sodium and chloride. Molecules can link up with one another to form yet another kind of building block known as a macromolecule. Macromolecules, present in the atmosphere of the young Earth, gave rise to cells, which in turn went on to form multicellular organisms; in forming those organisms, cells became a new kind of building block.

The Origin of Life

Molecules essential for life are thought to have formed spontaneously in the oceans of the primordial Earth about 4 billion years ago. Under the influence of a hot, stormy environment, the molecules combined to produce macromolecules, which in turn formed microscopic bubbles that were bounded by a sturdy macromolecular membrane analogous to the skin on a grape. It took about half a billion years for the prebiotic bubbles to evolve into the first cells, known as prokaryotes, and another 1 billion years for those cells to evolve into the eukaryotes. Prokaryotes, also known as bacteria, are small cells (about 5 micrometers in diameter) that have a relatively simple structure and a genome consisting of about 4,000 genes. Eukaryotes are much larger (about 30 micrometers in diameter), with a complex internal structure and a very large genome, often exceeding 20,000 genes. These genes are kept in a special organelle called the nucleus (eukaryote means "true nucleus"). Prokaryotes are all single-cell organisms, although some can form short chains or temporary fruiting bodies. Eukaryotes, on the other hand, gave rise to all of the multicellular plants and animals that now inhabit the Earth.

A Typical Eukaryote

Eukaryotes assume a variety of shapes that are variations on the simple spheres from which they originated. Viewed from the side, they often have a galactic profile, with a central bulge (the nucleus),

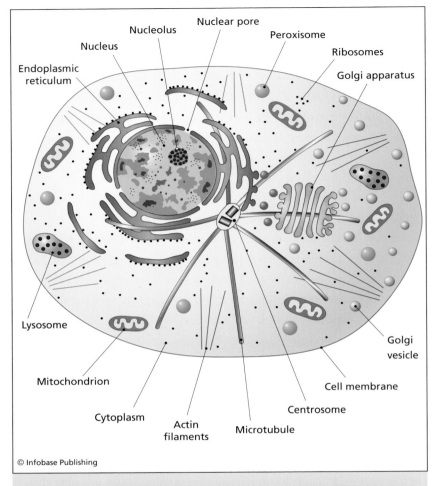

Nuclear pore
Nucleolus
Peroxisome
Nucleus
Ribosomes
Endoplasmic
reticulum
Golgi apparatus

Lysosome

Golgi
vesicle

Mitochondrion

Cell membrane

Cytoplasm

Centrosome

Actin
filaments

Microtubule

© Infobase Publishing

The eukaryote cell. The structural components shown here are present in organisms as diverse as protozoans, plants, and animals. The nucleus contains the DNA genome and an assembly plant for ribosomal subunits (the nucleolus). The endoplasmic reticulum (ER) and the Golgi work together to modify proteins, most of which are destined for the cell membrane. These proteins travel from the ER to the Golgi and from the Golgi to their final destination in transport vesicles (red and yellow spheres). Mitochondria provide the cell with energy in the form of ATP. Ribosomes, some of which are attached to the ER, synthesize proteins. Lysosomes and peroxisomes recycle cellular material. The microtubules and centrosome form the spindle apparatus for moving chromosomes to the daughter cells during cell division. Actin and other protein filaments form a weblike cytoskeleton.

tapering to a thin perimeter. The internal structure is complex, being dominated by a large number of organelles.

The functional organization of a eukaryote is analogous to a carpentry shop, which is usually divided into two main areas: the shop floor, where the machinery, building materials, and finishing rooms are kept; and the shop office, where the work is coordinated and where the blueprints are stored for everything the shop makes. Carpentry shops keep a blueprint on file for every item that is made. When the shop receives an order, perhaps for a chair, someone in the office makes a copy of the chair's blueprint and delivers it to the carpenters on the shop floor. In this way, the master copy is kept out of harm's way, safely stored in the filing cabinet. The carpenters, using the blueprint copy and the materials and tools at hand, build the chair, and then they send it into a special room where it is painted. After the chair is painted, it is taken to another room where it is polished and then packaged for delivery. The energy for all of this activity comes through the electrical wires, which are connected to a power generator somewhere in the local vicinity. The shop communicates with other shops and its customers by using the telephone, e-mail, or postal service.

In the cell the shop floor is called the cytoplasm, and the shop office is the nucleus. Eukaryotes make a large number of proteins, and they keep a blueprint for each one, only in this case the blueprints are not pictures on pieces of paper but molecules of deoxyribonucleic acid (DNA) that are kept in the nucleus. A cellular blueprint is called a gene, and a typical cell has thousands of them. A human cell, for example, has 30,000 genes, all of which are kept on 46 separate DNA molecules known as chromosomes (23 from each parent). When the cell decides to make a protein, it begins by making a ribonucleic acid (RNA) copy of the protein's gene. This blueprint copy, known as messenger RNA, is made in the nucleus and delivered to the cell's carpenters in the cytoplasm. These carpenters are enzymes that control and regulate all of the cell's chemical reactions. Some of the enzymes are part of a complex protein-synthesizing machine known as a ribosome. Cytoplasmic enzymes and the ribosomes synthesize proteins using mRNA as the template, after which many of the proteins are sent to a compartment, known as the endoplasmic reticulum (ER), where they are glycosylated, or "painted" with sugar molecules. From there they are shipped to another compartment called the Golgi apparatus, where the glycosylation is refined before the finished products, now looking like molecular trees, are loaded into transport bubbles and shipped to their final destination.

The shape of the cell is maintained by an internal cytoskeleton composed of actin and intermediate filaments. Mitochondria, once free-living prokaryotes, provide the cell with energy in the form of adenosine triphosphate (ATP). The production of ATP is carried out by an assembly of metal-containing proteins, called the electron transport chain, located in the mitochondrion inner membrane. Lysosomes and peroxisomes process and recycle cellular material and molecules. The cell communicates with other cells and the outside world through a forest of glycoproteins, known as the glycocalyx, that covers the cell surface. Producing and maintaining the glycocalyx is the principal function of the ER and Golgi apparatus and a major priority for all eukaryotes.

Cells are biochemical entities that synthesize many thousands of molecules. Studying these chemicals and the biochemistry of the cell would be extremely difficult were it not for the fact that most of the chemical variation is based on six types of molecules that are assembled into just five types of macromolecules. The six basic molecules are amino acids, phosphate, glycerol, sugars, fatty acids, and nucleotides. The five macromolecules are proteins, DNA, RNA, phospholipids, and sugar polymers called polysaccharides.

Molecules of the Cell

Amino acids have a simple core structure consisting of an amino group, a carboxyl group, and a variable R group attached to a carbon atom. There are 20 different kinds of amino acids, each with a unique R group. The simplest and most ancient amino acid is glycine, with an R group that consists only of hydrogen. The chemistry

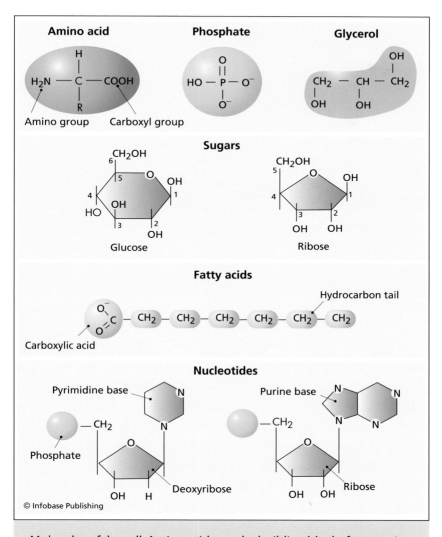

Molecules of the cell. Amino acids are the building blocks for proteins. Phosphate is an important component of many other molecules and is added to proteins to modify their behavior. Glycerol is an alcohol that is an important ingredient in cell membranes and fat. Sugars, like glucose, are a primary energy source for most cells and also have many structural functions. Fatty acids are involved in the production of cell membranes and storage of fat. Nucleotides are the building blocks for DNA and RNA. Note that the sugar carbon atoms are numbered. P: Phosphate, C: Carbon, H: Hydrogen, O: Oxygen, N: Nitrogen, R: Variable molecular group.

of the various amino acids varies considerably: Some carry a positive electric charge, while others are negatively charged or electrically neutral; some are water soluble (hydrophilic), while others are hydrophobic.

Phosphates are extremely important molecules that are used in the construction, or modification, of many other molecules. They are also used to store chemical-bond energy in the form of adenosine triphosphate (ATP). The production of phosphate-to-phosphate chemical bonds for use as an energy source is an ancient cellular process, dating back at least 2 billion years.

Glycerol is a simple three-carbon alcohol that is an important component of cell membranes and fat reservoirs. This molecule may have stabilized the membranes of prebiotic bubbles. Interestingly, it is often used today as an ingredient in a solution for making long-lasting soap bubbles.

Sugars are versatile molecules belonging to a general class of compounds known as carbohydrates that serve a structural role as well as providing energy for the cell. Glucose, a six-carbon sugar, is the primary energy source for most cells and the principal sugar used to glycosylate the proteins and lipids that form the outer coat of all cells. Plants have exploited the structural potential of sugars in their production of cellulose; wood, bark, grasses, and reeds are all polymers of glucose and other monosaccharides. Ribose, a five-carbon sugar, is a component of nucleic acids as well as the cell's main energy depot, ATP. The numbering convention for sugar carbon atoms is shown in the figure on page 135. Ribose carbons are numbered as 1′ (1 prime), 2′, and so on. Consequently, references to nucleic acids, which include ribose, often refer to the 3′ or 5′ carbon.

Fatty acids consist of a carboxyl group (the hydrated form is called carboxylic acid) linked to a hydrophobic hydrocarbon tail. These molecules are used in the construction of cell membranes and fat. The hydrophobic nature of fatty acids is critically important to the normal function of the cell membrane since it prevents the passive entry of water and water-soluble molecules.

Nucleotides are building blocks for DNA and RNA. These molecules consist of three components: a phosphate, a ribose sugar, and a nitrogenous (nitrogen-containing) ring compound that behaves as a base in solution (a base is a substance that can accept a proton in solution). Nucleotide bases appear in two forms: a single-ring nitrogenous base, called a pyrimidine, and a double-ringed base, called a purine. There are two kinds of purines (adenine and guanine) and three pyrimidines (uracil, cytosine, and thymine). Uracil is specific to RNA, substituting for thymine. In addition, RNA nucleotides contain ribose, whereas DNA nucleotides contain deoxyribose (hence the origin of their names). Ribose has a hydroxyl (OH) group attached to both the 2′ and 3′ carbons, whereas deoxyribose is missing the 2′ hydroxyl group.

Macromolecules of the Cell

The six basic molecules are used by all cells to construct five essential macromolecules: proteins, RNA, DNA, phospholipids, and polysaccharides. Macromolecules have primary, secondary, and tertiary structural levels. The primary structural level refers to the chain that is formed by linking the building blocks together. The secondary structure involves the bending of the linear chain to form a three-dimensional object. Tertiary structural elements involve the formation of chemical bonds between some of the building blocks in the chain to stabilize the secondary structure. A quaternary structure can also occur when two identical molecules interact to form a dimer or double molecule.

Proteins are long chains or polymers of amino acids. The primary structure is held together by peptide bonds that link the carboxyl end of one amino acid to the amino end of a second amino acid. Thus once constructed, every protein has an amino end and a carboxyl end. An average protein consists of about 400

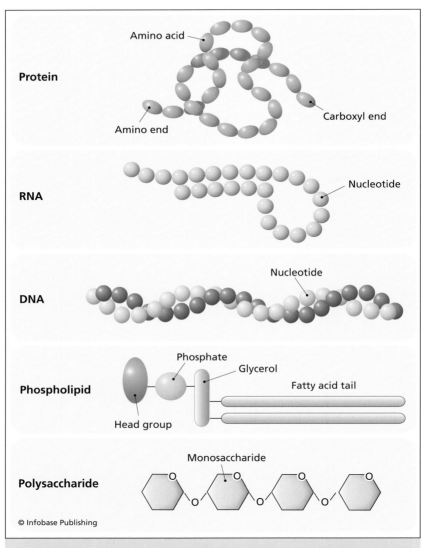

Macromolecules of the cell. Protein is made from amino acids linked together to form a long chain that can fold up into a three-dimensional structure. RNA and DNA are long chains of nucleotides. RNA is generally single-stranded, but can form localized double-stranded regions. DNA is a double-stranded helix, with one strand coiling around the other. A phospholipid is composed of a hydrophilic head-group, a phosphate, a glycerol molecule and two hydrophobic fatty acid tails. Polysaccharides are sugar polymers.

amino acids. There are 21 naturally occurring amino acids; with this number the cell can produce an almost infinite variety of proteins. Evolution and natural selection, however, have weeded out most of these, so that eukaryote cells function well with 10,000 to 30,000 different proteins. In addition, this select group of proteins has been conserved over the past 2 billion years (i.e., most of the proteins found in yeast can also be found, in modified form, in humans and other higher organisms). The secondary structure of a protein depends on the amino acid sequence and can be quite complicated, often producing three-dimensional structures possessing multiple functions.

Computer model of a molecule of the CD4 protein that plays a vital role in the immune system. Protein structural units are the colored balls, each color for a different amino acid. The CD4 protein, consisting of 450 amino acids, is found on the surface of white blood cells called T-helper cells. *(Dr. Tim Evans/Photo Researchers, Inc.)*

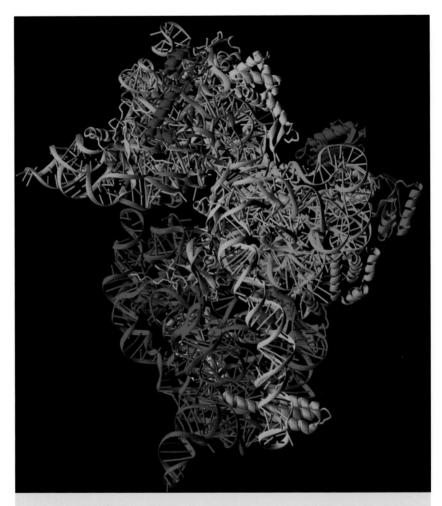

A model of DNA, looking down the long axis of the macromolecule
(Kenneth Eward/BioGrafx/Photo Researchers, Inc.)

RNA is a polymer of the ribonucleotides adenine, uracil, cytosine, and guanine. RNA is generally single-stranded, but it can form localized double-stranded regions by a process known as complementary base pairing, whereby adenine forms a bond with uracil and cytosine pairs with guanine. RNA is involved in the synthesis of proteins and is a structural and enzymatic component of ribosomes.

DNA is a double-stranded nucleic acid. This macromolecule encodes cellular genes and is constructed from adenine, thymine, cytosine, and guanine deoxyribonucleotides. The two DNA strands coil around each other like strands in a piece of rope, creating a double helix. The two strands are complementary throughout the length of the molecule: Adenine pairs with thymine, and cytosine pairs with guanine. Thus, if the sequence of one strand is known to be ATCGTC, the sequence of the other strand must be TAGCAG.

Phospholipids are the main component in cell membranes; these macromolecules are composed of a polar head group (usually an alcohol), a phosphate, glycerol, and two hydrophobic fatty acid tails. Fat that is stored in the body as an energy reserve has a structure similar to a phospholipid, being composed of three fatty acid chains attached to a molecule of glycerol. The third fatty acid takes the place of the phosphate and head group of a phospholipid.

Polysaccharides are sugar polymers consisting of two or more monosaccharides. Disaccharides (two monosaccharides) and oligosaccharides (about 3 to 12 monosaccharides) are attached to proteins and lipids destined for the cell surface or the extracellular matrix. Polysaccharides, such as glycogen and starch, may contain several hundred monosaccharides, and are stored in cells as an energy reserve.

Basic Cellular Functions

There are six basic cellular functions: DNA replication, DNA maintenance, gene expression, power generation, cell division, and cell communication. DNA replication usually occurs in conjunction with cell division, but there are exceptions known as polyploidization (see the glossary). Gene expression refers to the process whereby the information stored in a gene is used to synthesize RNA or protein. The production of power is accomplished by extracting energy from food molecules and then storing that energy in a form that is readily available to the cell. Cells communicate with their environment and with other cells. The communication hardware consists of a variety of special macromolecules that are embedded in the cell membrane.

DNA Replication

Replication is made possible by the complementarity of the two DNA strands. Since adenine (A) always pairs with thymine (T) and guanine (G) always pairs with cytosine (C), replication enzymes are able to duplicate the molecule by treating each of the original strands as templates for the new strands. For example, if a portion of the template strand reads ATCGTTGC, the new strand will be TAGCAACG.

DNA replication requires the coordinated effort of a team of enzymes, led by DNA helicase and primase. The helicase separates the two DNA strands at the astonishing rate of 1,000 nucleotides every second. This enzyme gets its name from the fact that it unwinds the DNA helix as it separates the two strands. The enzyme that is directly responsible for reading the template strand and for synthesizing the new daughter strand is called DNA polymerase. This enzyme also has an editorial function; it checks the preceding nucleotide to make sure it is correct before it adds a nucleotide to the growing chain. The editor function of this enzyme introduces an interesting problem. How can the polymerase add the very first nucleotide when it has to check a preceding nucleotide before adding a new one? A special enzyme, called primase, which is attached to the helicase, solves this problem. Primase synthesizes short pieces of RNA that form a DNA-RNA double-stranded region. The RNA becomes a temporary part of the daughter strand, thus priming the DNA polymerase by providing the crucial first nucleotide in the new strand. Once the chromosome is duplicated, DNA repair enzymes, discussed below, remove the RNA primers, and replace them with DNA nucleotides.

DNA Maintenance

Every day in a typical human cell thousands of nucleotides are being damaged by spontaneous chemical events, environmental pollutants, and radiation. In many cases, it takes only a single defective nucleotide within the coding region of a gene to produce an inactive, mutant protein. The most common forms of DNA damage are depurination and deamination. Depurination is the loss of a purine base (guanine or adenine) resulting in a gap in the DNA sequence, referred to as a "missing tooth." Deamination converts cytosine to uracil, a base that is normally found only in RNA.

About 5,000 purines are lost from each human cell every day, and over the same time period 100 cytosines are deaminated per cell. Depurination and deamination produce a great deal of damage, and in either case the daughter strand ends up with a missing nucleotide, and possibly a mutated gene, as the DNA replication machinery simply bypasses the uracil or the missing tooth. If left unrepaired, the mutated genes will be passed on to all daughter cells, with catastrophic consequences for the organism as a whole.

DNA damage caused by depurination is repaired by special nuclear proteins that detect the missing tooth, excise about 10 nucleotides on either side of the damage, and then, using the complementary strand as a guide, reconstruct the strand correctly. Deamination is dealt with by a special group of DNA repair enzymes known as base-flippers. These enzymes inspect the DNA one nucleotide at a time. After binding to a nucleotide, a base-flipper breaks the hydrogen bonds holding the nucleotide to its complementary partner. It then performs the maneuver for which it gets its name. Holding onto the nucleotide, it rotates the base a full 180 degrees, inspects it carefully, and, if it detects any damage, cuts the base out and discards it. In this case, the base-flipper leaves the final repair to the missing-tooth crew that detects and repairs the gap as described previously. If the nucleotide is normal, the base-flipper rotates it back into place and reseals the hydrogen bonds. Scientists have estimated that these maintenance crews inspect and repair the entire genome of a typical human cell in less than 24 hours.

Gene Expression

Genes encode proteins and several kinds of RNA. Extracting the coded information from DNA requires two sequential processes known as transcription and translation. A gene is said to be expressed when either or both of these processes have been completed. Transcription, catalyzed by the enzyme RNA polymerase, copies one strand of the DNA into a complementary strand of mRNA, which is sent to the cytoplasm, where it joins with a ribosome. Translation is a process that is orchestrated by the ribosomes. These particles synthesize proteins using mRNA and the genetic code as guides. The ribosome can synthesize any protein specified by the mRNA, and the mRNA can be translated many times before it is recycled. Some RNAs, such as ribosomal RNA and transfer RNA, are never translated. Ribosomal RNA (rRNA) is a structural and enzymatic component of ribosomes. Transfer RNA (tRNA), though separate from the ribosome, is part of the translation machinery.

The genetic code provides a way for the translation machinery to interpret the sequence information stored in the DNA molecule and represented by mRNA. DNA is a linear sequence of four different kinds of nucleotides, so the simplest code could be one in which each nucleotide specifies a different amino acid; that is, adenine coding for the amino acid glycine, cytosine for lysine, and so on. The earliest cells may have used this coding system, but it is limited to the construction of proteins consisting of only four different kinds of amino acids. Eventually, a more elaborate code evolved in which a combination of three out of the four possible DNA nucleotides, called codons, specifies a single amino acid. With this scheme it is possible to have a unique code for each of the 20 naturally occurring amino acids. For example, the codon AGC specifies the amino acid serine, whereas TGC specifies the amino acid cysteine. Thus a gene may be viewed as a long continuous sequence of codons. However, not all codons specify an amino acid. The sequence TGA signals the end of the gene, and a special codon, ATG, signals the start site, in addition to specifying the amino acid methionine. Consequently, all proteins begin with this amino acid, although it is sometimes removed once construction of the protein is complete. As mentioned above, an average protein may consist of 300 to 400 amino acids; since the codon consists of three nucleotides for each amino acid, a typical gene may be 900 to 1,200 nucleotides long.

Power Generation

Dietary fats, sugars, and proteins not targeted for growth, storage, or repairs are converted to ATP by the mitochondria. This process requires a number of metal-binding proteins, called the respiratory chain (also known as the electron transport chain), and a special ion channel-enzyme called ATP synthase. The respiratory chain consists of three major components: NADH dehydrogenase, cytochrome b, and cytochrome oxidase. All of these components are protein complexes with an iron (NADH dehydrogenase, cytochrome b) or a copper core (cytochrome oxidase), and together with the ATP synthase, are located in the inner membrane of the mitochondria.

The respiratory chain is analogous to an electric cable that transports electricity from a hydroelectric dam to our homes, where it is used to turn on lights or to run our stereos. The human body, like that of all animals, generates electricity by processing food molecules through a metabolic pathway called the Krebs cycle, also located within the mitochondria. The electrons (electricity) so generated are transferred to hydrogen ions, which quickly bind to a special nucleotide called nicotinamide adenine dinucleotide (NAD). Binding of the hydrogen ion to NAD is noted by abbreviating the resulting molecule as NADH. The electrons begin their journey down the respiratory chain when NADH binds to NADH dehydrogenase, the first component in the chain. This enzyme does just what its name implies: It removes the hydrogen from NADH, releasing the stored electrons, which are conducted through the chain by the iron and copper as though they were traveling along an electric wire. As the electrons travel from one end of the chain to the other, they energize the synthesis of ATP, which is released from the mitochondria for use by the cell. All electrical circuits must have a ground, that is, the electrons need someplace to go once they have completed the circuit. In the case of the respiratory chain, the ground is oxygen. After passing through cytochrome oxidase, the last component in the chain, the electrons are picked up by oxygen, which combines with hydrogen ions to form water.

The Cell Cycle

Free-living single cells divide as a way of reproducing their kind. Among plants and animals, cells divide as the organism grows from a seed, or an embryo, into a mature individual. This form of cell division, in which the parent cell divides into two identical daughter cells, is called mitosis. A second form of cell division, known as meiosis, is intended for sexual reproduction and occurs exclusively in gonads.

Cell division is part of a grander process known as the cell cycle, which consists of two phases: interphase and M phase (meiosis or mitosis). Interphase is divided into three sub-phases called Gap 1 (G_1), S phase (a period of DNA synthesis), and Gap 2 (G_2). The conclusion of interphase, and with it the termination of G_2, occurs with division of the cell and a return to G_1. Cells may leave the cycle by entering a special phase called G_0. Some cells, such as postmitotic neurons in an animal's brain, remain in G_0 for the life of the organism. For most cells the completion of the cycle, known as the generation time, can take 30 to 60 minutes.

Cells grow continuously during interphase while preparing for the next round of division. Two notable events are the

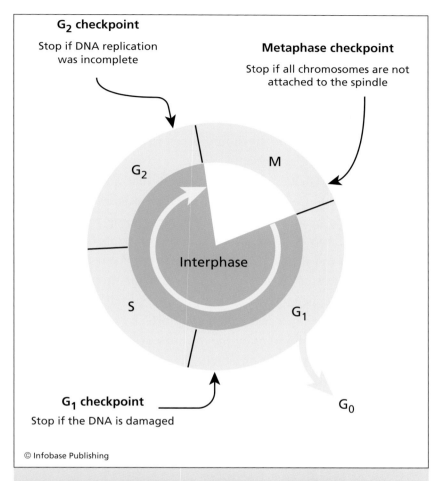

G$_2$ checkpoint

Stop if DNA replication
was incomplete

Metaphase checkpoint

Stop if all chromosomes are not
attached to the spindle

G$_2$

M

Interphase

S

G$_1$

G$_1$ checkpoint

Stop if the DNA is damaged

G$_0$

© Infobase Publishing

The cell cycle. Many cells spend their time cycling between inter-phase and M phase (cell division by mitosis or meiosis). Interphase is divided into three subphases: Gap 1 (G$_1$), S phase (DNA synthesis), and Gap 2 (G$_2$). Cells may exit the cycle by entering G$_0$. The cell cycle is equipped with three checkpoints to ensure the daughter cells are identical and that there is no genetic damage. The yellow arrow indicates the direction of the cycle.

duplication of the spindle (the centrosome and associated microtubules), a structure that is crucial for the movement of the chromosomes during cell division, and the appearance of an enzyme called maturation promoting factor (MPF) at the end of G$_2$.

MPF phosphorylates histones, proteins that bind to the DNA, and when phosphorylated compact (or condense) the chromosomes in preparation for cell division. MPF is also responsible for the breakdown of the nuclear membrane. When cell division is complete, MPF disappears, allowing the chromosomes to decondense and the nuclear envelope to reform. Completion of a normal cell cycle always involves the division of a cell into two daughter cells, either meiotically or mitotically.

Cell division is such a complex process that many things can, and do, go wrong. Cell cycle monitors, consisting of a team of enzymes, check to make sure that everything is going well each time a cell divides, and if it is not, those monitors stop the cell from dividing until the problem is corrected. If the damage cannot be repaired, a cell remains stuck in midstream for the remainder of its life. If this happens to a cell in an animal's body, it is forced to commit suicide, in a process called apoptosis, by other cells in the immediate neighborhood or by the immune system.

The cell cycle includes three checkpoints: The first is a DNA damage checkpoint that occurs in G_1. The monitors check for damage that may have occurred as a result of the last cell cycle or were caused by something in the environment, such as UV radiation or toxic chemicals. If damage is detected, DNA synthesis is blocked until it can be repaired. The second checkpoint occurs in G_2, where the monitors make sure errors were not introduced when the chromosomes were duplicated during S-phase. The G_1 and G_2 checkpoints are sometimes referred to collectively as DNA damage checkpoints. The third and final checkpoint occurs in M-phase to ensure that all of the chromosomes are properly attached to the spindle. This checkpoint is intended to prevent gross abnormalities in the daughter cells with regard to chromosome number. If a chromosome fails to attach to the spindle, one daughter cell will end up with too many chromosomes, while the other will have too few.

Mitosis

Mitosis is divided into four stages known as prophase, metaphase, anaphase, and telophase. The behavior and movement of the chromosomes characterize each stage. At prophase, DNA replication has already occurred, and the nuclear membrane begins to break down. Condensation of the duplicated chromosomes initiates the phase (i.e., the very long, thin chromosomes are folded up to produce short, thick chromosomes that are easy to move and maneuver). Under the microscope the chromosomes become visible as X-shaped structures, which are the two duplicated chromosomes, often called sister chromatids. A special region of each chromosome, called a centromere, holds the chromatids together. Proteins bind to the centromere to form a structure called the kinetochore. The centrosome is duplicated, and the two migrate to opposite ends of the cell.

During metaphase the chromosomes are sorted out and aligned between the two centrosomes. By this time the nuclear membrane has completely broken down. The two centrosomes and the microtubules fanning out between them form the mitotic spindle. The area in between the spindles, where the chromosomes are aligned, is known as the metaphase plate. Some of the microtubules make contact with the kinetochores, while others overlap, with motor proteins situated in between.

Anaphase begins when the duplicated chromosomes move to opposite poles of the cell. The first step is the release of an enzyme that breaks the bonds holding the kinetochores together, thus allowing the sister chromatids to separate from one another while remaining bound to their respective microtubules. Motor proteins, using energy supplied by ATP, move along the microtubule, dragging the chromosomes to opposite ends of the cell.

During telophase the daughter chromosomes arrive at the spindle poles and decondense to form the relaxed chromosomes characteristic of interphase nuclei. The nuclear envelope begins forming around the chromosomes, marking the end of mitosis. By the end of telophase, individual chromosomes are no longer distinguishable and are referred to as chromatin. While the nuclear membrane reforms, a contractile ring made of the proteins myosin and actin begins pinching the parental cell in two. This stage, separate from mitosis, is called cytokinesis, and leads to the formation of two daughter cells, each with one nucleus.

Meiosis

Many eukaryotes reproduce sexually through the fusion of gametes (eggs and sperm). If gametes were produced mitotically, a catastrophic growth in the number of chromosomes would occur each time a sperm fertilized an egg. Meiosis is a special form of cell division that prevents this from happening by producing haploid gametes, each possessing half as many chromosomes as the diploid cell. When haploid gametes fuse, they produce an embryo with the correct number of chromosomes.

Unlike mitosis, which produces two identical daughter cells, meiosis produces four genetically unique daughter cells that have half the number of chromosomes found in the parent cell. This is possible because meiosis consists of two rounds of cell division, called meiosis I and meiosis II, with only one round of DNA synthesis. Microbiologists discovered meiosis almost 100 years ago by comparing the number of chromosomes in somatic cells and germ cells. The roundworm, for example, was found to have four chromosomes in its somatic cells but only two in its gametes. Many other studies also compared the amount of DNA in nuclei from somatic cells and gonads, always with the same result: The amount of DNA in somatic cells is at least double the amount in fully mature gametes.

Meiotic divisions are divided into the four mitotic stages discussed above. Indeed, meiosis II is virtually identical to a mitotic division. Meiosis I resembles mitosis, but close examination shows two important differences: Gene swapping occurs between homologous chromosomes in prophase, producing recombinant chromosomes, and the distribution of maternal and paternal chromosomes to different daughter cells. At the end of meiosis I, one of the daughter cells contains a mixture of normal and recombinant maternal chromosomes, and the other contains normal and recombinant paternal chromosomes. During meiosis II, the duplicated chromosomes are distributed to different daughter cells, yielding four genetically unique cells: paternal, paternal recombinant, maternal, and maternal recombinant. Mixing genetic material in this way is unique to meiosis, and it is one of the reasons sexual reproduction has been such a powerful evolutionary force.

Cell Communication

A forest of glycoproteins and glycolipids covers the surface of every cell like trees on the surface of the Earth. The cell's forest is called the glycocalyx, and many of its trees function like sensory antennae. Cells use these antennae to communicate with their environment and with other cells. In multicellular organisms the glycocalyx also plays an important role in holding cells together. In this case, the antennae of adjacent cells are connected to one another through the formation of chemical bonds.

The sensory antennae, also known as receptors, are linked to a variety of secondary molecules that serve to relay messages to the interior of the cell. These molecules, some of which are called second messengers, may activate machinery in the cytoplasm, or they may enter the nucleus to activate gene expression. The signals that a cell receives are of many different kinds but generally fall into one of five categories: 1) proliferation, which stimulates the cell to grow and divide; 2) activation, which is a request for the cell to synthesize and release specific molecules; 3) deactivation, which serves as a brake for a previous activation signal; 4) navigation, which helps direct the cell to a specific location (this is very important for free-living cells hunting for food and for immune system cells that are hunting for invading microorganisms); 5) termination, which is a signal that orders the cell to commit suicide. This death signal occurs during embryonic development (e.g., the loss of webbing between the fingers and toes) and during an infection. In some cases, the only way the immune system can deal with an invading pathogenic microbe is to order some of the infected cells to commit suicide. This process is known as apoptosis.

BIOTECHNOLOGY

Biotechnology (also known as recombinant DNA technology) consists of several procedures that are used to study the structure and function of genes and their products. Central to this technology is the ability to clone specific pieces of DNA and to construct libraries of these DNA fragments that represent the genetic repertoire of an entire organism or a specific cell type. With these libraries at hand, scientists have been able to study the cell and whole organisms in unprecedented detail. The information so gained has revolutionized biology as well as many other disciplines, including medical science, pharmacology, psychiatry, and anthropology, to name but a few.

DNA Cloning

In 1973 scientists discovered that restriction enzymes (enzymes that can cut DNA at specific sites), DNA ligase (an enzyme that can join two pieces of DNA together), and bacterial plasmids could be used to clone DNA molecules. Plasmids are small (about 3,000 base pairs) circular minichromosomes that occur naturally in bacteria and are often exchanged between cells by passive diffusion. A bacterium is said to be transfected when it acquires a new plasmid. For bacteria, the main advantage to swapping plasmids is that they often carry antibiotic resistance genes, so that a cell sensitive to ampicillin can become resistant simply by acquiring the right plasmid. For scientists, plasmid swapping provided an ideal method for amplifying or cloning a specific piece of DNA.

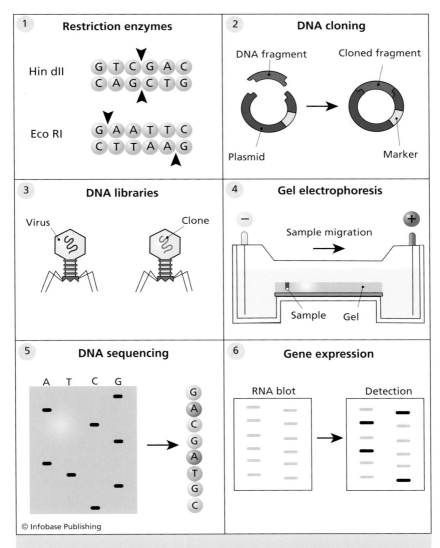

Biotechnology. This technology consists of six basic steps: 1) digestion of DNA with restriction enzymes in order to isolate specific DNA fragments; 2) cloning of restriction fragments in circular bacterial minichromosomes to increase their numbers; 3) storing the fragments for further study in viral-based DNA libraries; 4) isolation and purification of DNA fragments from gene libraries using gel electrophoresis; 5) sequencing cloned DNA fragments; 6) determining the expression profile of selected DNA clones using RNA blots and radioactive detection procedures.

The first cloning experiment used a plasmid from the bacterium *Escherichia coli* that was cut with the restriction enzyme *Eco*RI. The plasmid had a single *Eco*RI site so the restriction enzyme simply opened the circular molecule. Foreign DNA, cut with the same restriction enzyme, was incubated with the plasmid. Because the plasmid and foreign DNA were both cut with *Eco*RI, the DNA could insert itself into the plasmid to form a hybrid, or recombinant plasmid, after which DNA ligase sealed the two together. The reaction mixture was added to a small volume of *E. coli* so that some of the cells could take up the recombinant plasmid before being transferred to a nutrient broth containing streptomycin. Only those cells carrying the recombinant plasmid, which contained an antistreptomycin gene, could grow in the presence of this antibiotic. Each time the cells divided, the plasmid DNA was duplicated along with the main chromosome. After the cells had grown overnight, the foreign DNA had been amplified billions of times and was easily isolated for sequencing or expression studies. In this procedure the plasmid is known as a cloning vector because it serves to transfer the foreign DNA into a cell.

DNA Libraries

The basic cloning procedure described above not only provides a way to amplify a specific piece of DNA but also can be used to construct DNA libraries. In this case, however, the cloning vector is a bacteriophage called lambda. The lambda genome is double-stranded DNA of about 40,000 base pairs (bp), much of which can be replaced by foreign DNA without sacrificing the ability of the virus to infect bacteria. This is the great advantage of lambda over a plasmid. Lambda can accommodate very long pieces of DNA, often long enough to contain an entire gene, whereas a plasmid cannot accommodate foreign DNA that is larger than 2,000 base pairs. Moreover, bacteriophage has the natural ability to infect bacteria, so that the efficiency of transfection is 100 times greater than it is for plasmids.

The construction of a DNA library begins with the isolation of genomic DNA and its digestion with a restriction enzyme to produce fragments of 1,000 to 10,000 bp. These fragments are ligated into lambda genomes, which are subjected to a packaging reaction to produce mature viral particles, most of which carry a different piece of the genomic DNA. This collection of viruses is called a genomic library and is used to study the structure and organization of specific genes. Clones from a library such as this contain the coding sequences, in addition to noncoding sequences such as introns, intervening sequences, promoters, and enhancers. An alternative form of a DNA library can be constructed by isolating messenger RNA (mRNA) from a specific cell type. This RNA is converted to the complementary DNA (cDNA) using an RNA-dependent DNA polymerase called reverse transcriptase. The cDNA is ligated to lambda genomes and packaged as for the genomic library. This collection of recombinant viruses is known as a cDNA library and contains genes that were being expressed by the cells when the mRNA was extracted. It does not include introns or controlling elements, as these are lost during transcription and the processing that occurs in the cell to make mature mRNA. Thus a cDNA library is intended for the purpose of studying gene expression and the structure of the coding region only.

Labeling Cloned DNA

Many of the procedures used in biotechnology were inspired by the events that occur during DNA replication (described above). This includes the labeling of cloned DNA for use as probes in expression studies, DNA sequencing, and PCR (described below). DNA replication involves duplicating one of the strands (the parent, or template strand) by linking nucleotides in an order specified by the template and depends on a large number of enzymes, the most important of which is DNA polymerase. This enzyme, guided by the template strand, constructs a daughter strand by linking nucleotides together. One such nucleotide is deoxyadenine triphosphate (dATP). Deoxyribonucleotides have a single hydroxyl group located at the 3′ carbon of the sugar group while the triphosphate is attached to the 5′ carbon.

The procedure for labeling DNA probes, developed in 1983, introduces radioactive nucleotides into a DNA molecule. This method supplies DNA polymerase with a single-stranded DNA template, a primer, and the four nucleotides in a buffered solution to induce in vitro replication. The daughter strand, which becomes the labeled probe, is made radioactive by including a ^{32}P-labeled nucleotide in the reaction mix. The radioactive nucleotide is usually deoxycytosine triphosphate (dCTP) or dATP. The ^{32}P is always part of the α (alpha) phosphate (the phosphate closest to the 5′ carbon), as this is the one used by the polymerase to form the phosphodiester bond between nucleotides. Nucleotides can also be labeled with a fluorescent dye molecule.

Single-stranded DNA hexamers (six bases long) are used as primers, and these are produced in such a way that they contain all possible permutations of four bases taken six at a time. Randomizing the base sequence for the primers ensures that there will be at least one primer site in a template that is only 50 bp long. Templates used in labeling reactions such as this are generally 100 to 800 bp long. This strategy of labeling DNA is known as random primer labeling.

Gel Electrophoresis

This procedure is used to separate DNA and RNA fragments by size in a slab of agarose (highly refined agar) or polyacrylamide subjected to an electric field. Nucleic acids carry a negative charge and thus will migrate toward a positively charged electrode. The gel acts as a sieving medium that impedes the movement of the molecules. Thus the rate at which the fragments migrate is a function of their size; small fragments migrate more rapidly than large fragments.

The gel, containing the samples, is run submerged in a special pH-regulated solution, or buffer. Agarose gels are run horizontal as shown in the figure on page 153. But DNA sequencing gels, made of polyacrylamide, are much bigger and are run in a vertical tank.

DNA Sequencing

A sequencing reaction developed by the British biochemist Dr. Fred Sanger in 1976 is a technique that takes its inspiration from the natural process of DNA replication. DNA polymerase requires a primer with a free 3′ hydroxyl group. The polymerase adds the first nucleotide to this group, and all subsequent bases are added to the 3′ hydroxyl of the previous base. Sequencing by the Sanger method is usually performed with the DNA cloned into a special sequencing plasmid. This simplifies the choice of the primers since their sequence can be derived from the known plasmid sequence. Once the primer binds to the primer site, the cloned DNA may be replicated.

Sanger's innovation involved the synthesis of chain terminating nucleotide analogues lacking the 3′ hydroxyl group. These analogues, also known as dideoxynucleotides (ddATP, ddCTP, ddGTP and ddTTP), terminate the growth of the daughter strand at the point of insertion, and this can be used to determine the distance of each base on the daughter strand from the primer. These distances can be visualized by separating the Sanger reaction products on a poly-acrylamide gel, and then exposing the gel to X-ray film to produce an autoradiogram. The DNA sequence is read directly from this film, beginning with the smallest fragment at the bottom of the gel (the nucleotide closest to the primer) and ending with the largest fragment at the top. A hypothetical autoradiogram and the derived DNA sequence are shown in the figure (panel 5) on page 153. The smallest fragment in this example is the "C" nucleotide at the bottom of lane 3. The next nucleotide in the sequence is the "G" nucleotide in lane 4, then the "T" nucleotide in lane 2, and so on to the top of the gel.

Automated versions of the Sanger sequencing reaction use fluorescent-labeled dideoxynucleotides, each with a different color, so the sequence of the template can be recorded by a computer as the reaction mix passes a sensitive photocell. Machines such as this were used to sequence the human genome; a job that cost many millions of dollars and took years to complete. Recent advances in DNA sequencing technology will make it possible to sequence the human genome in less than a week at a cost of $1,000.

Gene Expression

The production of a genomic or cDNA library, followed by the sequencing of isolated clones, is a very powerful method for characterizing genes and the genomes from which they came. But the icing on the cake is the ability to determine the expression profile for a gene; that is, to determine which cells express the gene and exactly when the gene is turned on and off. Typical experiments may wish to determine the expression of specific genes in normal versus cancerous tissue, or tissues obtained from groups of different ages. There are essentially three methods for doing this: RNA blotting, fluorescent in situ hybridization (FISH), and the polymerase chain reaction.

RNA Blotting

This procedure consists of the following steps:

1. Extract mRNA from the cells or tissue of interest.
2. Fractionate (separate by size) the mRNA sample, using gel electrophoresis.
3. Transfer the fractionated sample to a nylon membrane (the blotting step).
4. Incubate the membrane with a gene fragment (usually a cDNA clone) that has been labeled with a radioisotope.
5. Expose the membrane to X-ray film to visualize the signal.

The RNA is transferred from the gel to a nylon membrane, using a vacuum apparatus or a simple dish containing a transfer buffer topped by a large stack of ordinary paper towels and a weight. The paper towels pull the transfer buffer through the gel, eluting the RNA from the gel and trapping it on the membrane. The location of specific mRNAs can be determined by hybridizing the membrane to a radiolabeled cDNA or genomic clone. The hybridization procedure involves placing the membrane in a buffer solution containing a labeled probe. During a long incubation period, the probe binds to the target sequence immobilized on the membrane. A-T and G-C base pairing (also known as hybridization) mediate the binding between the probe and target. The double-stranded molecule that is formed is a hybrid, being formed between the RNA target, on the membrane, and the DNA probe.

Fluorescent In Situ Hybridization (FISH)

Studying gene expression does not always depend on RNA blots and membrane hybridization. In the 1980s scientists found that cDNA probes could be hybridized to DNA or RNA in situ, that is, while located within cells or tissue sections fixed on a microscope slide. In this case, the probe is labeled with a fluorescent dye molecule, rather than a radioactive isotope. The samples are then examined and photographed under a fluorescent microscope. FISH is an extremely powerful variation on RNA blotting. This procedure gives precise information regarding the identity of a cell that expresses a specific gene, information that usually cannot be obtained with membrane hybridization. Organs and tissues are generally composed of many different kinds of cells, which cannot be separated from one another using standard biochemical extraction procedures. Histological sections, however, show clearly the various cell types, and when subjected to FISH analysis provide clear information as to which cells express specific genes. FISH is also used in clinical laboratories for the diagnosis of genetic abnormalities.

Polymerase Chain Reaction (PCR)

PCR is simply repetitive DNA replication over a limited, primer-defined, region of a suitable template. It provides a way of amplifying a short segment of DNA without going through the cloning procedures described above. The region defined by the primers is amplified to such an extent that it can be easily isolated for further study. The reaction exploits the fact that a DNA duplex, in a low-salt buffer, will melt (i.e., separate into two single strands) at 167°F (75°C), but will reanneal (rehybridize) at 98.6°F (37°C).

The reaction is initiated by melting the template, in the presence of primers and polymerase in a suitable buffer, cooling quickly to 98.6°F (37°C), and allowing sufficient time for the polymerase to replicate both strands of the template. The temperature is then increased to 167°F (75°C) to melt the newly formed duplexes and then cooled to 98.6°F (37°C). At the lower temperature, more primer will anneal to initiate another round of replication. The heating-cooling cycle is repeated 20 to 30 times, after which the reaction products are fractionated on an agarose gel, and the region containing the amplified fragment is cut out of the gel and purified for further study. The DNA polymerase used in these reactions is isolated from thermophilic bacteria that can withstand temperatures of 158°F (70°C) to 176°F (80°C). PCR applications are nearly limitless. It is used to amplify DNA from samples containing, at times, no more than a few cells. It is being used in the development of ultrafast DNA sequencers-identification of tissue samples in criminal investigations, amplification of ancient DNA obtained from fossils, and the identification of genes that are turned on or off during embryonic development, or during cellular transformation (cancer formation).

THE HUMAN GENOME PROJECT

Sequencing the entire human genome is an idea that grew over a period of 20 years, beginning in the early 1980s. At that time the

Sanger sequencing method was but a few years old and had only been used to sequence viral or mitochondrial genomes. Indeed, one of the first genomes to be sequenced was that of bacteriophage G4, a virus that infects the bacterium *Escherichia coli (E. coli)*. The G4 genome consists of 5,577 nucleotide pairs (or base pairs, abbreviated bp) and was sequenced in Sanger's laboratory in 1979. By 1982 the Sanger protocol was used by others to sequence the genome of the animal virus SV40 (5,224 bp), the human mitochondrion (16,569 bp), and bacteriophage lambda (48,502 bp). Besides providing invaluable data, these projects demonstrated the feasibility of sequencing very large genomes.

The possibility of sequencing the entire human genome was first discussed at scientific meetings organized by the U.S. Department of Energy (DOE) between 1984 and 1986. A committee appointed by the U.S. National Research Council endorsed the idea in 1988 but recommended a broader program to include the sequencing of the genes of humans, bacteria, yeast, worms, flies, and mice. They also called for the establishment of research programs devoted to the ethical, legal, and social issues raised by human genome research. The program was formally launched in late 1990 as a consortium consisting of coordinated sequencing projects in the United States, Britain, France, Germany, Japan, and China. At about the same time, the Human Genome Organization (HUGO) was founded to provide a forum for international coordination of genomic research.

By 1995 the consortium had established a strategy, called hierarchical shotgun sequencing, which they applied to the human genome as well as to the other organisms mentioned. With this strategy genomic DNA is cut into one-megabase (Mb) fragments (i.e., each fragment consists of 1 million bases) that are cloned into bacterial artificial chromosomes (BACs) to form a library of DNA fragments. The BAC fragments are partially characterized, then organized into an overlapping assembly called a contig. Clones are selected from the contigs for shotgun sequencing. That is, each shotgun clone is digested into small 1,000 bp fragments, sequenced, and then assembled into the final sequence with the aid of computers. Organizing the initial BAC fragments into contigs greatly simplifies the final assembly stage.

Sequencing of the human genome was divided into two stages. The first stage, completed in 2001, was a rough draft that covered about 80 percent of the genome with an estimated size of more than 3 billion bases (also expressed as 3 gigabases, or 3 Gb). The final draft, completed in April 2003, covers the entire genome and refines the data for areas of the genome that were difficult to sequence. It also filled in many gaps that occurred in the rough draft. The final draft of the human genome gives us a great deal of information that may be divided into three categories: gene content, gene origins, and gene organization.

Gene Content

Analysis of the final draft has shown that the human genome consists of 3.2 Gb of DNA, encoding about 30,000 genes (estimates range between 25,000 to 32,000). Functions are known for only half of these genes. With an average size of 3,000 bases, the genes occupy only about 2 percent of the DNA, a result that was both unexpected and baffling. The human genome appears to be much larger than it needs to be. The vast regions of noncoding DNA, known as intervening sequences, have been the subject of much study and speculation. Some researchers believe that these regions do nothing at all and have taken to calling them "junk DNA." More creative minds have suggested that the intervening sequences are involved in the control of gene expression, the maintenance of chromosome structure, and the protection of genes from insertional mutagenesis.

The estimated number of genes in the human genome is another surprising result. Some scientists, noting the complexity of our brains and physiology, had predicted it would be closer to 100,000 genes. By comparison, the fruit fly has 13,338 genes, and

THE GENOMES OF SOME ANIMALS, PLANTS, AND MICROBES

ORGANISM	GENOME SIZE (BP)	NUMBER OF GENES
Human	3.2 billion	30,000
Laboratory mouse	2.6 billion	25,000
Mustard weed	100 million	25,000
Corn	2.5 billion	50,000
Roundworm	97 million	18,266
Fruit fly	137 million	13,338
Yeast	12.1 million	6,000
Bacterium	4.6 million	3,200
Human immuno-deficiency virus	9,700	9

the simple roundworm, *Caenorhabditis elegans (C. elegans),* has 18,266. These numbers seemed absurd because they were so close to that of humans. But on reflection, the genome data suggests that human complexity, as compared to the fruit fly or the worm, is not simply due to the absolute number of genes but involves the complexity of the proteins that are encoded by those genes. In general, human proteins tend to be much more complex than those of lower organisms. Data from the final draft and other sources also provides a detailed overview of the functional profile of human cellular proteins.

Gene Origins

Fully one half of human genes originated as transposable elements, also known as jumping genes (described below). Equally surprising is the fact that 220 of our genes were obtained by horizontal transfer from bacteria, rather than by ancestral, or vertical, inheritance. In other words, humans have obtained genes directly from bacteria, probably mediated by viral infections in a kind of natural gene therapy or gene swapping. Researchers know this to be the case because while these genes occur in bacteria, they are not present in yeast, fruit flies, or eukaryotes that have been tested.

The function of most of the horizontally transferred genes is unclear, although a few may code for basic metabolic enzymes. A notable exception is the *MAO* gene that codes for an enzyme called monoamine oxidase (MAO). Note that by convention, gene names are written in upper or lowercase italic, while the proteins are uppercase Roman. Monoamines are neurotransmitters, such as dopamine, norepinephrine, and serotonin, which are needed for neural signaling in the human central nervous system. Monoamine oxidase plays a crucial role in the turnover of these neurotransmitters. How *MAO,* obtained from bacteria, could have developed such an important role in human physiology is a great mystery.

Gene Organization

In prokaryotes (bacteria), genes are simply arranged in tandem along a single chromosome, with little if any DNA separating one gene from the other. Each gene is transcribed into messenger RNA, which is translated into protein. Indeed, in prokaryotes, which have no nucleus, translation often begins even before transcription is complete. In eukaryotes, as one might expect, gene organization is more complex. Data from the genome project shows clearly that eukaryote genes are split into subunits, called exons, and that each exon is separated by a length of DNA called an intron. A gene, consisting of introns and exons, is separated from other genes by the intervening sequences. Eukaryote genes are transcribed into a primary RNA molecule that includes exon and intron sequences. The primary transcript never leaves the nucleus and is never translated into protein. Nuclear enzymes remove the introns from the primary transcript, after which the exons are joined together to form the mature mRNA. Thus only the exons carry the necessary code to produce a protein.

THE BELMONT REPORT

On July 12, 1975, the American National Research Act was signed into law, thereby creating a national commission to protect human research subjects. This commission was charged with the task of identifying basic ethical principles that should govern the conduct of any research involving human subjects, and in February 1976 the commission produced the Belmont Report (so named because the report was finalized at the Smithsonian Institution's Belmont Conference Center). The report began by defining three basic ethical principles that should be applied to research involving human subjects: the principles of respect for persons, beneficence, and justice.

Respect for Persons

Respect for persons demands that subjects enter into research voluntarily and with adequate information. This assumes the individuals are autonomous agents, that is, are competent to make up their own minds. However, there are many instances where potential research subjects are not really autonomous: prisoners, patients in a mental institution, children, the elderly and the infirm. All of these people require special protection to ensure they are not being coerced or fooled into volunteering as research subjects. The subjects in the Tuskegee study were all poor, uneducated farm workers who were especially vulnerable to coercion.

Beneficence

Beneficence is generally regarded as acts of kindness or charity, but the report insisted that in the case of research subjects, it be made an obligation. In this sense, it is the natural extension of the

Hippocratic oath that all physicians are expected to adhere by: *I will give no deadly medicine to anyone if asked, nor suggest any such counsel.* In other words, physicians should do no harm, and those involved in biomedical research should never injure one person to benefit another.

Justice

Justice is an extension of beneficence. Researchers must never enlist subjects in an experiment if those subjects do not stand to reap any benefits. The exploitation of prisoners in Nazi concentration camps benefited the Nazis, but certainly not the people they experimented on. A second example cited by the Belmont Report was the Tuskegee study. Aside from committing a gross deviation from the most basic of ethical standards, the designers of the Tuskegee study enlisted only black people even though they are not the only racial group to suffer from the disease under study. The principle of justice was clearly not applied to these subjects.

Guided by these three ethical principles, the report introduced the following requirements that all human research trials must adhere to: informed consent, risk/benefit assessment, and fair selection of research subjects.

Informed Consent

All participants must provide informed consent, in writing. Moreover, steps must be taken to ensure the consent is in fact informed. This might involve an independent assessment of the individual's ability to understand the language on the consent form, as well as any instructions or explanations the investigators have given. Since the Gelsinger investigation, this process was amended to include a patient advocate, present at any meeting between the physicians and the prospective volunteers. This has the added advantage of ensuring that in a case where the patient is fully competent, the scientists do not give them misleading or inaccurate information or try to coerce them in any way.

Risk/Benefit Assessment

There is no point in having an ethical standard based on doing no harm if there is no formalized method available for assessing the risk to patient. It is the risk that is paramount in a patient's mind. No matter how grand the possible benefits, few would volunteer if they thought they would die as a consequence. The only exception to this might be terminally ill patients who volunteer for a clinical trial, even though they know they are not likely survive it. Independent committees based on information supplied by the investigators monitor risk assessment. In general, risks should be reduced to those necessary to achieve the research objective. If there is significant risk, review committees are expected to demand a justification for it.

Selection of Subjects

The selection process must be fair. Low-risk, potentially beneficial research should not be offered to one segment of society, while high-risk research is conducted on prisoners, low-income groups, or anyone in a disadvantaged social position.

Conclusions

The Belmont Report introduced, for the first time, the principle of informed consent. Backing this up is the recommendation for independent review committees that ensure the ethical guidelines are being followed. In the United States, the FDA and NIH are responsible for enforcing the guidelines laid out by the Belmont Report. There are, in addition, local review committees (called institutional review boards) that must approve any experimentation using human subjects. The Belmont Report was inspired by the general public's anger over the Tuskegee study. It is fitting that on May 16, 1997, the surviving members of the Tuskegee study were invited to the White House, where President Bill Clinton issued a formal apology and reaffirmed the nation's commitment to rigorous ethical standards in biomedical research. No one would have believed at the time that further trouble was just around the corner.

THE GELSINGER INVESTIGATION

In fall 1998 a gene therapy trial to treat a liver disease was begun at the University of Pennsylvania. The investigators recruited 18 patients, and the 18th patient, who happened to be 18 years of age, was Jesse Gelsinger. Gelsinger joined the trial on September 13, 1999. On the second day of his treatment, he lapsed into a coma, and was pronounced dead 24 hours later. Within days of Gelsinger's death, the National Institutes of Health (NIH) ordered a halt to all American gene therapy trials that were using a similar research protocol. The ban was to last a full year and was accompanied by an investigation that was not concluded until fall 2001.

The team leader of the clinical trial, Dr. James Wilson, reported Gelsinger's death immediately. A preliminary review was conducted from November 30, 1999, to January 19, 2000. The full review was to last for more than a year and covered every aspect of Dr. Wilson's protocol and the criteria used to admit patients to the trial. In January 2000 NIH released preliminary results of their investigation, which cited the principal investigators for failure to adhere to the clinical protocol and an apparent disregard for the safety of the study subjects. The report focused on four main points: failure to adhere to the stopping rules, failure to adhere to the principle of informed consent, failure to keep adequate records regarding vector lineage and titer, and changing the protocol without approval.

Failure to Adhere to the Stopping Rules

The study was designed around several cohorts that were treated in tandem so that in the event of toxic reactions in one cohort treatment the study could be terminated before other cohorts were treated. However, toxic reactions observed in five of the cohorts did not lead to termination of the trial before Gelsinger was treated. Many of the patients suffered harsher reactions to the treatment than was expected, and this should have been sufficient reason to stop the trial. In addition, most of the toxic reactions experienced by the patients in this study were never reported to the FDA or NIH. In the months following the conclusion of the Gelsinger preliminary investigation, other investigations showed that failure to report toxic reactions was a common failure in many gene therapy trials. In one study, the patients experienced 691 serious side effects, and of these, only 39 were reported as required by the federal agencies.

Failure to Adhere to the Principle of Informed Consent

When a toxic response occurred in cohort 1, cohort 2 should have been informed of this response to give those patients the option of withdrawing from the study. This was not done. Moreover, the investigators discovered that none of the subjects were told about adverse effects on monkeys in the preclinical trial. One of the monkeys received the same virus used in the clinical trial, though at a higher dose, and within a week of being treated it was euthanized because it developed the same clotting disorder that killed Gelsinger. Since the subjects were not told about this, the consent forms were ruled invalid. It was this charge that led to the call for a patient advocate in all future biomedical research trials, regardless of their nature.

Failure to Keep Adequate Records Regarding Vector Lineage and Titer

This was an especially damaging finding since it implied that the researchers gave Gelsinger more virus than they thought they had. The term *titer* refers to the number of vector particles in a given solution. Determining the titer is not straightforward, and if errors are made, the concentration may be out in increments of 10, rather than double or triple the amount expected. The possibility that Gelsinger was accidentally given a higher than stated dose is suggested by the fact that a woman in his cohort received a nearly identical dose (3.0×10^{13}) without signs of liver damage or multiorgan failure. As mentioned above, a monkey in a preclinical trial received a higher dose ($17\times$ greater) of the same virus and subsequently died of multiorgan failure. If there was an error made in calculating the dose for Gelsinger, it is possible he received an equivalent, fatal amount.

Changing the Protocol without Approval

The most serious infraction here had to do with the ammonia levels in the blood of prospective volunteers. As laid out in the original protocol, patients having more that 50 micromoles of ammonia per milliliter of blood were barred from volunteering because such a test result indicates severe liver damage. This was increased, sometime after the trial began, to 70 micromoles, without formal approval from the FDA. Gelsinger's ammonia level on the day he was treated was about 60 micromoles. If the original cutoff had been adhered to, he would have been excluded from the study. This is another indication of how important it is to adhere to the principle of informed consent and to the inclusion of an independent patient advocate.

UNDERSTANDING CLINICAL TRIALS

Clinical trials are conducted in four phases and are always preceded by research conducted on experimental animals such as mice, rats, or monkeys. The format for preclinical research is informal; it is conducted in a variety of research labs around the world, with the results being published in scientific journals. Formal approval from a governmental regulatory body is not required.

Phase I Clinical Trial

Pending the outcome of the preclinical research, investigators may apply for permission to try the experiments on human subjects. Applications in the United States are made to the Food and Drug Administration (FDA), the National Institutes of Health (NIH), and the Recombinant DNA Advisory Committee (RAC). RAC was set up by NIH to monitor any research, including clinical trials, dealing with cloning, recombinant DNA, or gene therapy. Phase I trials are conducted on a small number of adult volunteers, usually between two and 20, who have given informed consent. That is, the investigators explain the procedure, the possible outcomes, and especially, the dangers associated with the procedure before the subjects sign a consent form. The purpose of the Phase I trial is to determine the overall effect the treatment has on humans. A treatment that works well in monkeys or mice may not work at all on humans. Similarly, a treatment that appears safe in lab animals may be toxic, even deadly, when given to humans. Since most clinical trials are testing a new drug of some kind, the first priority is to determine a safe dosage for humans. Consequently, subjects in the Phase I trial are given a range of doses, all of which, even the high dose, are less than the highest dose given to experimental animals. If the results from the Phase I trial are promising, the investigators may apply for permission to proceed to Phase II.

Phase II Clinical Trial

Having established the general protocol, or procedure, the investigators now try to replicate the encouraging results from Phase I, but with a much larger number of subjects (100–300). Only with a large number of subjects is it possible to prove the treatment has an effect. In addition, dangerous side effects may have been missed in Phase I because of a small sample size. The results from Phase II will determine how safe the procedure is and whether it works or not. If the statistics show the treatment is effective, and toxicity is low, the investigators may apply for permission to proceed to Phase III.

Phase III Clinical Trial

Based on Phase II results, the procedure may look very promising, but before it can be used as a routine treatment it must be tested on thousands of patients at a variety of research centers. This is the expensive part of bringing a new drug or therapy to market, costing millions, sometimes billions, of dollars. It is for this reason that Phase III clinical trials invariably have the financial backing of large pharmaceutical or biotechnology companies. If the results of the Phase II trial are confirmed in Phase III, the FDA will approve the use of the drug for routine treatment. The use of the drug or treatment now passes into an informal Phase IV trial.

Phase IV Clinical Trial

Even though the treatment has gained formal approval, its performance is monitored for very long-term effects, sometimes stretching on for 10 to 20 years. In this way, the FDA retains the power to recall the drug long after it has become a part of standard medical procedure. It can happen that in the long term, the drug costs more than an alternative, in which case, health insurance providers may refuse to cover the cost of the treatment.

GENE AND PROTEIN NOMENCLATURE

Scientists who were, in effect, probing around in the dark have discovered many genes and their encoded proteins. Once discovered, the new genes or proteins had to be named. Usually the "name" is nothing more than a lab-book code or an acronym suggested by the system under study at the time. Sometimes it turns out, after further study, that the function observed in the original study is a minor aspect of the gene's role in the cell. It is for this reason that gene and protein names sometimes seem absurd and poorly chosen.

In 2003 an International Committee on Standardized Genetic Nomenclature agreed to unify the rules and guidelines for gene and protein names for the mouse and rat. Similar committees have attempted to standardize gene-naming conventions for human, frog, zebrafish, and yeast genes. In general, the gene name is expected to be brief and to begin with a lowercase letter unless it is a person's name. The gene symbols are acronyms taken from the gene name and are expected to be three to five characters long and not more than 10. The symbols must be written with Roman letters and Arabic numbers. The same symbol is used for orthologs (i.e., the same gene) among different species, such as human, mouse, or rat. Thus the gene sonic hedgehog is symbolized as shh, and the gene myelocytomatosis is symbolized as myc.

Unfortunately, the various committees were unable to agree on a common presentation for the gene and protein symbols. A human gene symbol, for example, is italicized, uppercase letters and the protein is uppercase and not italicized. A frog gene symbol is lower-case, and the protein is uppercase, while neither is italicized. Thus the myc gene and its protein, for example, are written as *MYC* and MYC in humans, myc and MYC in frogs, and *Myc* and Myc in mice and rats. The later convention, *Myc* and Myc is used throughout the New Biology set, regardless of the species.

WEIGHTS AND MEASURES

The following table presents some common weights, measures, and conversions that appear in this book.

QUANTITY	EQUIVALENT
Length	1 meter (m) = 100 centimeters (cm) = 1.094 yards = 39.37 inches 1 kilometer (km) = 1,000 m = 0.62 miles 1 foot = 30.48 cm 1 inch = 1/12 foot = 2.54 cm 1 cm = 0.394 inch = 10^{-2} (or 0.01) m 1 millimeter (mm) = 10^{-3} m 1 micrometer (μm) = 10^{-6} m 1 nanometer (nm) = 10^{-9} m 1 Ångström (Å) = 10^{-10} m
Mass	1 gram (g) = 0.0035 ounce 1 pound = 16 ounces = 453.6 grams 1 kilogram (kg) = 2.2 pounds (lb) 1 milligram (mg) = 10^{-3} g 1 microgram (μg) = 10^{-6} g
Volume	1 liter (l) = 1.06 quarts (US) = 0.264 gallon (US) 1 quart (US) = 32 fluid ounces = 0.95 liter 1 milliliter (ml) = 10^{-3} liter = 1 cubic centimeter (cc)
Temperature	°C = 5/9 (°F - 32) °F = (9/5 × °C) + 32
Energy	Calorie = the amount of heat needed to raise the temperature of 1 gram of water by 1°C. Kilocalorie = 1,000 calories. Used to describe the energy content of foods.

Glossary

acetyl A chemical group derived from acetic acid that is important in energy metabolism and for the modification of proteins.

acetylcholine A neurotransmitter released at axonal terminals by cholinergic neurons, found in the central and peripheral nervous systems and released at the vertebrate neuromuscular junction.

acetyl-CoA A water-soluble molecule, coenzyme A (CoA) that carries acetyl groups in cells.

acid A substance that releases protons when dissolved in water; carries a net negative charge.

actin filament A protein filament formed by the polymerization of globular actin molecules; forms the cytoskeleton of all eukaryotes and part of the contractile apparatus of skeletal muscle.

action potential A self-propagating electrical impulse that occurs in the membranes of neurons, muscles, photoreceptors, and hair cells of the inner ear.

active transport Movement of molecules across the cell membrane, using the energy stored in ATP.

adenylate cyclase A membrane-bound enzyme that catalyzes the conversion of ATP to cyclic AMP; an important component of cell-signaling pathways.

adherens junction A cell junction in which the cytoplasmic face of the membrane is attached to actin filaments.

adipocyte A fat cell.

adrenaline (epinephrine) A hormone released by chromaffin cells in the adrenal gland; prepares an animal for extreme activity by increasing the heart rate and blood sugar levels.

adult stem cells   Stem cells isolated from adult tissues, such as bone marrow or epithelium.

aerobic   Refers to a process that either requires oxygen or occurs in its presence.

agar   A polysaccharide isolated from seaweed that forms a gel when boiled in water and cooled to room temperature; used by microbiologists as a solid culture medium for the isolation and growth of bacteria and fungi.

agarose   A purified form of agar that is used to fractionate (separate by size) biomolecules.

allele   An alternate form of a gene. Diploid organisms have two alleles for each gene, located at the same locus (position) on homologous chromosomes.

allogeneic transplant   A cell, tissue, or organ transplant from an unrelated individual.

alpha helix   A common folding pattern of proteins in which a linear sequence of amino acids twists into a right-handed helix stabilized by hydrogen bonds.

amino acid   An organic molecule containing amino and carboxyl groups that is a building block of protein.

aminoacyl tRNA   An amino acid linked by its carboxyl group to a hydroxyl group on tRNA.

aminoacyl-tRNA synthetase   An enzyme that attaches the correct amino acid to a tRNA.

amino terminus   The end of a protein or polypeptide chain that carries a free amino group.

amphipathic   Having both hydrophilic and hydrophobic regions, as in a phospholipid.

anabolism   A collection of metabolic reactions in a cell whereby large molecules are made from smaller ones.

anaerobic   A cellular metabolism that does not depend on molecular oxygen.

anaphase   A mitotic stage in which the two sets of chromosomes move away from each other toward opposite spindle poles.

anchoring junction   A cell junction that attaches cells to each other.

angiogenesis   Sprouting of new blood vessels from preexisting ones.

angstrom   A unit of length, equal to 10^{-10} meter or 0.1 nanometer (nM), that is used to measure molecules and atoms.

anterior   A position close to or at the head end of the body.

antibiotic   A substance made by bacteria, fungi, and plants that is toxic to microorganisms. Common examples are penicillin and streptomycin.

antibody   A protein made by B cells of the immune system in response to invading microbes.

anticodon   A sequence of three nucleotides in tRNA that is complementary to a messenger RNA codon.

antigen   A molecule that stimulates an immune response, leading to the formation of antibodies.

antigen-presenting cell   A cell of the immune system, such as a monocyte, that presents pieces of an invading microbe (the antigen) to lymphocytes.

antiparallel   The relative orientation of the two strands in a DNA double helix; the polarity of one strand is oriented in the opposite direction to the other.

antiporter   A membrane carrier protein that transports two different molecules across a membrane in opposite directions.

apoptosis   Regulated or programmed form of cell death that may be activated by the cell itself or by the immune system to force cells to commit suicide when they become infected with a virus or bacterium.

archaea   The archaea are prokaryotes that are physically similar to bacteria (both lack a nucleus and internal organelles), but they have retained a primitive biochemistry and physiology that would have been commonplace 2 billion years ago.

asexual reproduction   The process of forming new individuals without gametes or the fertilization of an egg by a sperm. Individuals produced this way are identical to the parent and referred to as a clone.

aster   The star-shaped arrangement of microtubules that is characteristic of a mitotic or meiotic spindle.

ATP (adenosine triphosphate)   A nucleoside consisting of adenine, ribose, and three phosphate groups that is the main carrier of chemical energy in the cell.

ATPase   Any enzyme that catalyzes a biochemical reaction by extracting the necessary energy from ATP.

ATP synthase   A protein located in the inner membrane of the mitochondrion that catalyzes the formation of ATP from ADP and inorganic phosphate using the energy supplied by the electron transport chain.

autogeneic transplant   A patient receives a transplant of his or her own tissue.

autologous   Refers to tissues or cells derived from the patient's own body.

autoradiograph (autoradiogram)   X-ray film that has been exposed to X-rays or to a source of radioactivity; used to visualize internal structures of the body and radioactive signals from sequencing gels and DNA or RNA blots.

autosome   Any chromosome other than a sex chromosome.

axon   A long extension of a neuron's cell body that transmits an electrical signal to other neurons.

axonal transport   The transport of organelles, such as Golgi vesicles, along an axon to the axonal terminus. Transport also flows from the terminus to the cell body.

bacteria   One of the most ancient forms of cellular life (the other is the archaea). Bacteria are prokaryotes, and some are known to cause disease.

bacterial artificial chromosome (BAC)   A cloning vector that accommodates DNA inserts of up to 1 million base pairs.

bacteriophage   A virus that infects bacteria. Bacteriophages were used to prove that DNA is the cell's genetic material and are now used as cloning vectors.

base   A substance that can accept a proton in solution. The purines and pyrimidines in DNA and RNA are organic bases and are often referred to simply as bases.

base pair   Two nucleotides in RNA or DNA that are held together by hydrogen bonds. Adenine bound to thymine or guanine bound to cytosine are examples of base pairs

B cell (B lymphocyte)   A white blood cell that makes antibodies and is part of the adaptive immune response.

benign   Tumors that grow to a limited size and do not spread to other parts of the body.

beta sheet   Common structural motif in proteins in which different strands of the protein run alongside one another and are held together by hydrogen bonds.

biopsy   The removal of cells or tissues for examination under a microscope. When only a sample of tissue is removed, the procedure is called an incisional biopsy or core biopsy. When an entire lump or suspicious area is removed, the procedure is called an excisional biopsy. When a sample of tissue or fluid is removed with a needle, the procedure is called a needle biopsy or fine-needle aspiration.

biosphere   The world of living organisms

biotechnology   A set of procedures that are used to study and manipulate genes and their products.

blastomere   A cell formed by the cleavage of a fertilized egg. Blastomeres are the totipotent cells of the early embryo.

blotting   A technique for transferring DNA (southern blotting), RNA (northern blotting), or proteins (western blotting) from an agarose or polyacrylamide gel to a nylon membrane.

BRCA1 (breast cancer gene 1)   A gene on chromosome 17 that may be involved in regulating the cell cycle. A person who inherits an altered version of the BRCA1 gene has a higher risk of getting breast, ovarian, or prostate cancer.

BRCA2 (breast cancer gene 2)   A gene on chromosome 13 that, when mutated, increases the risk of getting breast, ovarian, or prostate cancer.

budding yeast   The common name for the baker's yeast *Saccharomyces cerevisiae,* a popular experimental organism that reproduces by budding off a parental cell.

buffer   A pH-regulated solution with a known electrolyte (salt) content; used in the isolation, manipulation, and storage of biomolecules and medicinal products.

cadherin   Belongs to a family of proteins that mediates cell-cell adhesion in animal tissues.

calorie   A unit of heat. One calorie is the amount of heat needed to raise the temperature of one gram of water by 1°C. kilocalories (1,000 calories) are used to describe the energy content of foods.

capsid   The protein coat of a virus, formed by autoassembly of one or more proteins into a geometrically symmetrical structure.

carbohydrate   A general class of compounds that includes sugars, containing carbon, hydrogen, and oxygen.

carboxyl group   A carbon atom attached to an oxygen and a hydroxyl group

carboxyl terminus   The end of a protein containing a carboxyl group.

carcinogen   A compound or form of radiation that can cause cancer.

carcinogenesis   The formation of a cancer.

carcinoma   Cancer of the epithelium, representing the majority of human cancers.

cardiac muscle   Muscle of the heart; composed of myocytes that are linked together in a communication network based on free passage of small molecules through gap junctions.

caspase   A protease involved in the initiation of apoptosis.

catabolism   Enzyme regulated breakdown of large molecules for the extraction of chemical-bond energy. Intermediate products are called catabolites.

catalyst   A substance that lowers the activation energy of a reaction.

CD28   Cell-surface protein located in T-cell membranes, necessary for the activation of T-cells by foreign antigens.

cDNA (complementary DNA)   DNA that is synthesized from mRNA, thus containing the complementary sequence; cDNA contains coding sequence, but not the regulatory sequences that are present in the genome. Labeled probes are made from cDNA for the study of gene expression.

cell adhesion molecule (CAM)   A cell surface protein that is used to connect cells to one another.

cell body   The main part of a cell containing the nucleus, Golgi complex, and endoplasmic reticulum; used in reference to neurons that have long processes (dendrites and axons) extending some distance from the nucleus and cytoplasmic machinery.

cell coat   (see **glycocalyx**)

cell-cycle control system   A team of regulatory proteins that governs progression through the cell cycle.

cell-division-cycle gene (*cdc* gene)   A gene that controls a specific step in the cell cycle.

cell fate   The final differentiated state that a pluripotent embryonic cell is expected to attain.

cell-medicated immune response   Activation of specific cells to launch an immune response against an invading microbe.

cell nuclear transfer   Animal cloning technique whereby a somatic cell nucleus is transferred to an enucleated oocyte; synonymous with somatic cell nuclear transfer.

celsius   A measure of temperature. This scale is defined such that 0°C is the temperature at which water freezes and 100°C is the temperature at which water boils.

central nervous system (CNS)   That part of a nervous system that analyzes signals from the body and the environment. In animals, the CNS includes the brain and spinal cord.

centriole   A cylindrical array of microtubules that is found at the center of a centrosome in animal cells.

centromere   A region of a mitotic chromosome that holds sister chromatids together. Microtubules of the spindle fiber connect to an area of the centromere called the kinetochore.

centrosome   Organizes the mitotic spindle and the spindle poles; in most animal cells it contains a pair of centrioles.

chiasma (plural chiasmata)   An X-shaped connection between homologous chromosomes that occurs during meiosis I, representing a site of crossing-over, or genetic exchange between the two chromosomes.

chromatid   A duplicate chromosome that is still connected to the original at the centromere. The identical pair are called sister chromatids.

chromatin   A complex of DNA and proteins (histones and non-histones) that forms each chromosome and is found in the nucleus of all eukaryotes. Decondensed and threadlike during interphase.

chromatin condensation   Compaction of different regions of interphase chromosomes that is mediated by the histones.

chromosome   One long molecule of DNA that contains the organism's genes. In prokaryotes, the chromosome is circular and naked; in eukaryotes, it is linear and complexed with histone and nonhistone proteins.

chromosome condensation Compaction of entire chromosomes in preparation for cell division.

clinical breast exam An exam of the breast performed by a physician to check for lumps or other changes.

cnidoblast A stinging cell found in the Cnidarians (jellyfish).

cyclic adenosine monophosphate (cAMP) A second messenger in a cell-signaling pathway that is produced from ATP by the enzyme adenylate cyclase.

cyclin A protein that activates protein kinases (cyclin-dependent protein kinases, or Cdk) that control progression from one stage of the cell cycle to another.

cytochemistry The study of the intracellular distribution of chemicals.

cytochrome Colored, iron-containing protein that is part of the electron transport chain.

cytotoxic T cell A T lymphocyte that kills infected body cells.

dendrite An extension of a nerve cell that receives signals from other neurons.

dexrazoxane A drug used to protect the heart from the toxic effects of anthracycline drugs such as doxorubicin. It belongs to the family of drugs called chemoprotective agents.

dideoxynucleotide A nucleotide lacking the 2' and 3' hydroxyl groups.

dideoxy sequencing A method for sequencing DNA that employs dideoxyribose nucleotides; also known as the Sanger sequencing method, after Fred Sanger, a chemist who invented the procedure in 1976.

diploid A genetic term meaning two sets of homologous chromosomes, one set from the mother and the other from the father. Thus, diploid organisms have two versions (alleles) of each gene in the genome.

DNA (deoxyribonucleic acid) A long polymer formed by linking four different kinds of nucleotides together likes beads on a string. The sequence of nucleotides is used to encode an organism's genes.

DNA helicase An enzyme that separates and unwinds the two DNA strands in preparation for replication or transcription.

DNA library A collection of DNA fragments that are cloned into plasmids or viral genomes.

DNA ligase   An enzyme that joins two DNA strands together to make a continuous DNA molecule.

DNA microarray   A technique for studying the simultaneous expression of a very large number of genes.

DNA polymerase   An enzyme that synthesizes DNA using one strand as a template.

DNA primase   An enzyme that synthesizes a short strand of RNA that serves as a primer for DNA replication.

dorsal   The backside of an animal; also refers to the upper surface of anatomical structures, such as arms or wings.

dorsalventral   The body axis running from the backside to the frontside or the upperside to the underside of a structure.

double helix   The three-dimensional structure of DNA in which the two strands twist around each other to form a spiral.

doxorubicin   An anticancer drug that belongs to a family of antitumor antibiotics.

Drosophila melanogaster   Small species of fly, commonly called a fruit fly, that is used as an experimental organism in genetics, embryology, and gerontology.

ductal carcinoma in situ (DCIS)   Abnormal cells that involve only the lining of a breast duct. The cells have not spread outside the duct to other tissues in the breast; also called intraductal carcinoma.

dynein   A motor protein that is involved in chromosome movements during cell division.

dysplasia   Disordered growth of cells in a tissue or organ, often leading to the development of cancer.

ectoderm   An embryonic tissue that is the precursor of the epidermis and the nervous system.

electrochemical gradient   A differential concentration of an ion or molecule across the cell membrane that serves as a source of potential energy and may polarize the cell electrically.

electron microscope   A microscope that uses electrons to produce a high-resolution image of the cell.

electrophoresis   The movement of a molecule, such as protein, DNA, or RNA, through an electric field. In practice, the molecules migrate through a slab of agarose or polyacrylamide that is immersed in a special solution and subjected to an electric field.

elution   To remove one substance from another by washing it out with a buffer or solvent.

embryogenesis   The development of an embryo from a fertilized egg.

embryonic stem cell (ES cell)   A pluripotent cell derived from the inner cell mass (the cells that give rise to the embryo instead of the placenta) of a mammalian embryo.

endocrine cell   A cell that is specialized for the production and release of hormones. Such cells make up hormone-producing tissue such as the pituitary gland or gonads.

endocytosis   Cellular uptake of material from the environment by invagination of the cell membrane to form a vesicle called an endosome. The endosome's contents are made available to the cell after it fuses with a lysosome.

endoderm   An embryonic tissue layer that gives rise to the gut.

endoplasmic reticulum (ER)   Membrane-bounded chambers that are used to modify newly synthesized proteins with the addition of sugar molecules (glycosylation). When finished, the glycosylated proteins are sent to the Golgi apparatus in exocytotic vesicles.

enhancer   A DNA-regulatory sequence that provides a binding site for transcription factors capable of increasing the rate of transcription for a specific gene; often located thousands of base pairs away from the gene it regulates.

enveloped virus   A virus containing a capsid that is surrounded by a lipid bilayer originally obtained from the membrane of a previously infected cell.

enzyme   A protein or RNA that catalyzes a specific chemical reaction.

epidermis   The epithelial layer, or skin, that covers the outer surface of the body.

ER marker sequence   The amino terminal sequence that directs proteins to enter the endoplasmic reticulum (ER). This sequence is removed once the protein enters the ER.

erythrocyte   A red blood cell that contains the oxygen-carrying pigment hemoglobin; used to deliver oxygen to cells in the body.

***Escherichia coli* (E. coli)**   Rod-shape, gram-negative bacterium that inhabits the intestinal tract of most animals and is used as an experimental organism by geneticists and biomedical researchers.

euchromatin   Lightly staining portion of interphase chromatin, in contrast to the darkly staining heterochromatin (condensed chromatin). Euchromatin contains most, if not all, of the active genes.

eukaryote (eucaryote)   A cell containing a nucleus and many membrane-bounded organelles. All life-forms, except bacteria and viruses, are composed of eukaryote cells.

exocytosis   The process by which molecules are secreted from a cell. Molecules to be secreted are located in Golgi-derived vesicles that fuse with the inner surface of the cell membrane, depositing the contents into the intercellular space.

exon   Coding region of a eukaryote gene that is represented in messenger RNA and thus directs the synthesis of a specific protein.

expression studies   Examination of the type and quantity of mRNA or protein that is produced by cells, tissues, or organs.

fat   A lipid material, consisting of triglycerides (fatty acids bound to glycerol), that is stored adipocytes as an energy reserve.

fatty acid   A compound that has a carboxylic acid attached to a long hydrocarbon chain. A major source of cellular energy and a component of phospholipids.

fertilization   The fusion of haploid male and female gametes to form a diploid zygote.

fibroblast   The cell type that, by secreting an extracellular matrix, gives rise to the connective tissue of the body.

Filopodium   A fingerlike projection of a cell's cytoplasmic membrane, commonly observed in amoeba and embryonic nerve cells.

filter hybridization   The detection of specific DNA or RNA molecules, fixed on a nylon filter (or membrane), by incubating the filter with a labeled probe that hybridizes to the target sequence; also known as membrane hybridization.

fixative   A chemical that is used to preserve cells and tissues. Common examples are formaldehyde, methanol, and acetic acid.

flagellum (plural flagella)   Whiplike structure found in prokaryotes and eukaryotes that are used to propel cells through water.

fluorescein   Fluorescent dye that produces a green light when illuminated with ultraviolet or blue light.

fluorescent dye   A dye that absorbs UV or blue light and emits light of a longer wavelength, usually as green or red light.

fluorescent in situ hybridization (FISH)   A procedure for detecting the expression of a specific gene in tissue sections or smears through the use of DNA probes labeled with a fluorescent dye.

fluorescent microscope   A microscope that is equipped with special filters and a beam splitter for the examination of tissues and cells stained with a fluorescent dye.

follicle cell   Cells that surround and help feed a developing oocyte.

G_0 G "zero" refers to a phase of the cell cycle; state of withdrawal from the cycle as the cell enters a resting or quiescent stage; occurs in differentiated body cells, as well as in developing oocytes.

G_1 Gap 1 refers to the phase of the cell cycle that occurs just after mitosis and before the next round of DNA synthesis.

G_2 The Gap 2 phase of the cell cycle follows DNA replication and precedes mitosis.

gap junction   A communication channel in the membranes of adjacent cells that allows free passage of ions and small molecules.

gel electrophoresis   A procedure that is used to separate biomolecules by forcing them to migrate through a gel matrix (agarose or polyacrylamide) subjected to an electric field.

gene   A region of the DNA that specifies a specific protein or RNA molecule that is handed down from one generation to the next. This region includes both the coding, noncoding, and regulatory sequences.

gene regulatory protein   Any protein that binds to DNA and thereby affects the expression of a specific gene.

gene repressor protein   A protein that binds to DNA and blocks transcription of a specific gene.

gene therapy   A method for treating disease whereby a defective gene, causing the disease, is either repaired, replaced, or supplemented with a functional copy.

genetic code   A set of rules that assigns a specific DNA or RNA triplet, consisting of a three-base sequence, to a specific amino acid.

genome   All of the genes that belong to a cell or an organism.

genomic library   A collection of DNA fragments, obtained by digesting genomic DNA with a restriction enzyme, that are cloned into plasmid or viral vectors.

genomics   The study of DNA sequences and their role in the function and structure of an organism.

genotype   The genetic composition of a cell or organism.

germ cell   Cells that develop into gametes, either sperm or oocytes.

glucose   Six-carbon monosaccharide (sugar) that is the principal source of energy for many cells and organisms; stored as glycogen in animal cells and as starch in plants. Wood is an elaborate polymer of glucose and other sugars.

glycerol   A three-carbon alcohol that is an important component of phospholipids.

glycocalyx   A molecular "forest," consisting of glycosylated proteins and lipids, that covers the surface of every cell. The glycoproteins and glycolipids, carried to the cell membrane by Golgi-derived vesicles, have many functions including the formation of ion channels, cell-signaling receptors, and transporters.

glycogen   A polymer of glucose, used to store energy in an animal cell.

glycolysis   The degradation of glucose with production of ATP.

glycoprotein   Any protein that has a chain of glucose molecules (oligo-saccharide) attached to some of the amino acid residues.

glycosylation   The process of adding one or more sugar molecules to proteins or lipids.

glycosyltransferase   An enzyme in the Golgi complex that adds glucose to proteins.

Golgi complex (Golgi apparatus)   Membrane-bounded organelle in eukaryote cells that receives glycoproteins from the ER, which are modified and sorted before being sent to their final destination. The Golgi complex is also the source of glycolipids that are destined for the cell membrane. The glycoproteins and glycolipids leave the Golgi by exocytosis. This organelle is named after the Italian histologist Camillo Golgi, who discovered it in 1898.

Gram stain   A bacterial stain that detects different species of bacteria based on the composition of their cell wall. Bacteria that retain the Gram stain are colored blue (Gram positive), whereas those that do not are colored orange (Gram negative).

granulocyte   A type of white blood cell that includes the neutrophils, basophils, and eosinophils.

growth factor   A small protein (polypeptide) that can stimulate cells to grow and proliferate.

haploid   Having only one set of chromosomes; a condition that is typical in gametes, such as sperm and eggs.

HeLa cell   A tumor-derived cell line, originally isolated from a cancer patient in 1951; currently used by many laboratories to study the cell biology of cancer and carcinogenesis.

helix-loop-helix   A structural motif common to a group of gene-regulatory proteins.

helper T cell   A type of T lymphocyte that helps stimulate B cells to make antibodies directed against a specific microbe or antigen.

hemoglobin   An iron-containing protein complex, located in red blood cells, that picks up oxygen in the lungs and carries it to other tissues and cells of the body.

hemopoiesis   Production of blood cells, occurring primarily in the bone marrow.

hematopoietic   Refers to cells, derived form the bone marrow, that give rise to red and white blood cells.

hematopoietic stem cell transplantation (HSCT)   The use of stem cells isolated from the bone marrow to treat leukemia and lymphoma.

hepatocyte   A liver cell.

heterochromatin   A region of a chromosome that is highly condensed and transcriptionally inactive.

histochemistry   The study of chemical differentiation of tissues.

histology   The study of tissues.

histone   Small nuclear proteins, rich in the amino acids arginine and lysine, that form the nucleosome in eukaryote nuclei, a beadlike structure that is a major component of chromatin.

HIV   The human immunodeficiency virus that is responsible for AIDS.

homolog   One of two or more genes that have a similar sequence and are descended from a common ancestor gene.

homologous   Organs or molecules that are similar in structure because they have descended from a common ancestor; used primarily in reference to DNA and protein sequences.

homologous chromosomes   Two copies of the same chromosome, one inherited from the mother and the other from the father.

hormone   A signaling molecule, produced and secreted by endocrine glands; usually released into general circulation for coordination of an animal's physiology.

housekeeping gene   A gene that codes for a protein that is needed by all cells, regardless of the cell's specialization. Genes encoding enzymes involved in glycolysis and Krebs cycle are common examples.

hybridization   A term used in molecular biology (recombinant DNA technology) meaning the formation a double-stranded nucleic acid through complementary base-pairing; a property that is exploited in filter hybridization; a procedure that is used to screen gene libraries and to study gene structure and expression.

hydrolysis   The breaking of a covalent chemical bond with the subsequent addition of a molecule of water.

hydrophilic   A polar compound that mixes readily with water.

hydrophobic   A nonpolar molecule that dissolves in fat and lipid solutions, but not in water.

hydroxyl group (-OH)   Chemical group consisting of oxygen and hydrogen that is a prominent part of alcohol.

image analysis   A computerized method for extracting information from digitized microscopic images of cells or cell organelles.

immunofluorescence   Detection of a specific cellular protein with the aid of a fluorescent dye that is coupled to an antibody.

immunoglobulin (Ig)   An antibody made by B cells as part of the adaptive immune response.

incontinence   Inability to control the flow of urine from the bladder (urinary incontinence) or the escape of stool from the rectum (fecal incontinence).

insertional mutagenesis   Damage suffered by a gene when a virus or a jumping gene inserts itself into a chromosome.

in situ hybridization   A method for studying gene expression, whereby a labeled cDNA or RNA probe hybridizes to a specific mRNA in intact cells or tissues. The procedure is usually carried out on tissue sections or smears of individual cells.

insulin   Polypeptide hormone secreted by β (beta) cells in the vertebrate pancreas. Production of this hormone is regulated directly by the amount of glucose that is in the blood.

interleukin   A small protein hormone, secreted by lymphocytes, to activate and coordinate the adaptive immune response.

interphase   The period between each cell division, which includes the G_1, S, and G_2 phases of the cell cycle.

intron   A section of a eukaryotic gene that is noncoding. It is transcribed but does not appear in the mature mRNA.

in vitro   Refers to cells growing in culture or a biochemical reaction occurring in a test tube (Latin for "in glass").

in vivo   A biochemical reaction, or a process, occurring in living cells or a living organism (Latin for "in life").

ion   An atom that has gained or lost electrons, thus acquiring a charge. Common examples are Na^+ and Ca^{++} ions.

ion channel   A transmembrane channel that allows ions to diffuse across the membrane down their electrochemical gradient.

ischemia   An inadequate supply of blood to a part of the body caused by degenerative vascular disease.

Jak-STAT signaling pathway   One of several cell signaling pathways that activates gene expression. The pathway is activated through cell surface receptors and cytoplasmic Janus kinases (Jaks) and signal transducers and activators of transcription (STATs).

karyotype   A pictorial catalogue of a cell's chromosomes, showing their number, size, shape, and overall banding pattern.

keratin   Proteins produced by specialized epithelial cells called keratinocytes. Keratin is found in hair, fingernails, and feathers.

kilometer   1,000 meters, which is equal to 0.621 miles.

kinesin   A motor protein that uses energy obtained from the hydrolysis of ATP to move along a microtubule.

kinetochore   A complex of proteins that forms around the centromere of mitotic or meiotic chromosomes, providing an attachment site for microtubules. The other end of each microtubule is attached to a chromosome.

Krebs cycle (citric acid cycle)   The central metabolic pathway in all eukaryotes and aerobic prokaryotes; discovered by the German chemist Hans Krebs in 1937. The cycle oxidizes acetyl groups derived from food molecules. The end products are CO_2, H_2O, and high-energy electrons, which pass via NADH and FADH2 to the respiratory chain. In eukaryotes, the Krebs cycle is located in the mitochondria.

labeling reaction   The addition of a radioactive atom or fluorescent dye to DNA or RNA for use as a probe in filter hybridization.

lagging strand   One of the two newly synthesized DNA strands at a replication fork. The lagging strand is synthesized discontinuously and therefore its completion lags behind the second, or leading, strand.

lambda bacteriophage   A viral parasite that infects bacteria; widely used as a DNA cloning vector.

leading strand   One of the two newly synthesized DNA strands at a replication fork. The leading strand is made by continuous synthesis in the 5' to 3' direction.

leucine zipper   A structural motif of DNA binding proteins, in which two identical proteins are joined together at regularly spaced leucine residues, much like a zipper, to form a dimer.

leukemia   Cancer of white blood cells.

lipid bilayer   Two closely aligned sheets of phospholipids that form the core structure of all cell membranes. The two layers are aligned such that the hydrophobic tails are interior, while the hydrophilic head groups are exterior on both surfaces.

liposome   An artificial lipid bilayer vesicle used in membrane studies and as an artificial gene therapy vector.

locus   A term from genetics that refers to the position of a gene along a chromosome. Different alleles of the same gene occupy the same locus.

long-term potentiation (LTP)   A physical remodeling of synaptic junctions that receive continuous stimulation.

lumen   A cavity completely surrounded by epithelial cells.

lymphocyte   A type of white blood cell that is involved in the adaptive immune response. There are two kinds of lymphocytes: T lymphocytes and B lymphocytes. T lymphocytes (T cells) mature in the thymus and attack invading microbes directly. B lymphocytes (B cells) mature in the bone marrow and make antibodies that are designed to immobilize or destroy specific microbes or antigens.

lysis   The rupture of the cell membrane followed by death of the cell.

lysosome   Membrane-bounded organelle of eukaryotes that contains powerful digestive enzymes.

macromolecule   A very large molecule that is built from smaller molecular subunits. Common examples are DNA, proteins, and polysaccharides.

magnetic resonance imaging (MRI)   A procedure in which radio waves and a powerful magnet linked to a computer are used to create detailed pictures of areas inside the body. These pictures can show the difference between normal and diseased tissue. MRI makes better images of organs and soft tissue than other scanning techniques, such as CT or X-ray. MRI is especially useful for imaging the brain, spine, the soft tissue of joints, and the inside of bones. Also called nuclear magnetic resonance imaging.

major histocompatibility complex   Vertebrate genes that code for a large family of cell-surface glycoproteins that bind foreign antigens and present them to T cells to induce an immune response.

malignant   Refers to the functional status of a cancer cell that grows aggressively and is able to metastasize, or colonize, other areas of the body.

mammography   The use of X-rays to create a picture of the breast.

MAP-kinase (mitogen-activated protein kinase)   A protein kinase that is part of a cell proliferation–inducing signaling pathway.

M-cyclin   A eukaryote enzyme that regulates mitosis.

meiosis   A special form of cell division by which haploid gametes are produced. This is accomplished with two rounds of cell division, but only one round of DNA replication.

melanocyte   A skin cell that produces the pigment melanin.

membrane   The lipid bilayer and the associated glycocalyx that surround and enclose all cells.

membrane channel   A protein complex that forms a pore or channel through the membrane for the free passage of ions and small molecules.

membrane potential   A buildup of charged ions on one side of the cell membrane establishes an electrochemical gradient that is measured in millivolts (mV); an important characteristic of neurons as it provides the electrical current, when ion channels open, that enable these cells to communicate with one another.

mesoderm   An embryonic germ layer that gives rise to muscle, connective tissue, bones, and many internal organs.

messenger RNA (mRNA)   An RNA transcribed from a gene that is used as the gene template by the ribosomes and other components of the translation machinery to synthesize a protein.

metabolism   The sum total of the chemical processes that occur in living cells.

metaphase   The stage of mitosis at which the chromosomes are attached to the spindle but have not begun to move apart.

metaphase plate   Refers to the imaginary plane established by the chromosomes as they line up at right angles to the spindle poles.

metaplasia   A change in the pattern of cellular behavior that often precedes the development of cancer.

metastasis   Spread of cancer cells from the site of the original tumor to other parts of the body.

meter   Basic unit in the metric system; equal to 39.4 inches or 1.09 yards.

methyl group (-CH$_3$)   Hydrophobic chemical group derived from methane; occurs at the end of a fatty acid.

micrograph   Photograph taken through a light, or electron, microscope.

micrometer (μm or micron)   Equal to 10^{-6} meters.

microtubule   A fine cylindrical tube made of the protein tubulin, forming a major component of the eukaryote cytoskeleton.

millimeter (mm)   Equal to 10^{-3} meters.

mitochondrion (plural mitochondria)   Eukaryote organelle, formerly free living, that produces most of the cell's ATP.

mitogen   A hormone or signaling molecule that stimulates cells to grow and divide.

mitosis   Division of a eukaryotic nucleus; from the Greek *mitos,* meaning a thread, in reference to the threadlike appearance of interphase chromosomes.

mitotic chromosome   Highly condensed duplicated chromosomes held together by the centromere. Each member of the pair is referred to as a sister chromatid.

mitotic spindle   Array of microtubules, fanning out from the polar centrioles, and connecting to each of the chromosomes.

molecule   Two or more atoms linked together by covalent bonds.

monoclonal antibody   An antibody produced from a B cell–derived clonal line. Since all of the cells are clones of the original B cell, the antibodies produced are identical.

monocyte   A type of white blood cell that is involved in the immune response.

motif   An element of structure or pattern that may be a recurring domain in a variety of proteins.

M phase   The period of the cell cycle (mitosis or meiosis) when the chromosomes separate and migrate to the opposite poles of the spindle.

multipass transmembrane protein   A membrane protein that passes back and forth across the lipid bilayer.

multipotency   The property by which an undifferentiated animal cell can give rise to many of the body's cell types.

mutant   A genetic variation within a population.

mutation   A heritable change in the nucleotide sequence of a chromosome.

myelin sheath   Insulation applied to the axons of neurons. The sheath is produced by oligodendrocytes in the central nervous system and by Schwann cells in the peripheral nervous system.

myeloid cell   White blood cells other than lymphocytes.

myoblast   Muscle precursor cell; many myoblasts fuse into a syncytium, containing many nuclei, to form a single muscle cell.

myocyte   A muscle cell.

NAD (nicotine adenine dinucleotide)   Accepts a hydride ion (H^-), produced by the Krebs cycle, forming NADH, the main carrier of electrons for oxidative phosphorylation.

NADHdehydrogenase   Removes electrons from NADH and passes them down the electron transport chain.

nanometer (nm)   Equal to 10^{-9} meters or 10^{-3} microns.

National Institutes of Health (NIH)   A biomedical research center that is part of the U.S. Department of Health and Human Services. NIH consists of more than 25 research institutes, including the National Institute of Aging (NIA) and the National Cancer Institute (NCI). All of the institutes are funded by the federal government.

natural killer cell (NK cell)   A lymphocyte that kills virus-infected cells in the body; also kills foreign cells associated with a tissue or organ transplant.

neuromodulator   A chemical released by neurons at a synapse that modifies the behavior of the targeted neuron(s).

neuromuscular junction   A special form of synapse between a motor neuron and a skeletal muscle cell.

neuron   A cell specially adapted for communication that forms the nervous system of all animals.

neurotransmitter   A chemical released by the synapse that activates the targeted neuron.

non–small cell lung cancer   A group of lung cancers that includes squamous cell carcinoma, adenocarcinoma, and large cell carcinoma. The small cells are endocrine cells.

northern blotting   A technique for the study of gene expression. Messenger RNA (mRNA) is fractionated on an agarose gel and then transferred to a piece of nylon filter paper (or membrane). A specific mRNA is detected by hybridization with a labeled DNA or RNA probe. The original blotting technique invented by E. M. Southern inspired the name. Also known as RNA blotting.

nuclear envelope   The double membrane (two lipid bilayers) enclosing the cell nucleus.

nuclear localization signal (NLS)   A short amino acid sequence located on proteins that are destined for the cell nucleus, after they are translated in the cytoplasm.

nuclei acid   DNA or RNA, a macromolecule consisting of a chain of nucleotides.

nucleolar organizer   Region of a chromosome containing a cluster of ribosomal RNA genes that gives rise to the nucleolus.

nucleolus   A structure in the nucleus where ribosomal RNA is transcribed and ribosomal subunits are assembled.

nucleoside   A purine or pyrimidine linked to a ribose or deoxyribose sugar.

nucleosome   A beadlike structure, consisting of histone proteins.

nucleotide   A nucleoside containing one or more phosphate groups linked to the 5′ carbon of the ribose sugar. DNA and RNA are nucleotide polymers.

nucleus   Eukaryote cell organelle that contains the DNA genome on one or more chromosomes.

oligodendrocyte   A myelinating glia cell of the vertebrate central nervous system.

oligo labeling   A method for incorporating labeled nucleotides into a short piece of DNA or RNA. Also known as the random-primer labeling method.

oligomer   A short polymer, usually consisting of amino acids (oligopeptides), sugars (oligosaccharides), or nucleotides (oligonucleotides); taken from the Greek word *oligos,* meaning few or little.

oncogene　A mutant form of a normal cellular gene, known as a proto-oncogene, that can transform a cell to a cancerous phenotype.

oocyte　A female gamete or egg cell.

operator　A region of a prokaryote chromosome that controls the expression of adjacent genes.

operon　Two or more prokaryote genes that are transcribed into a single mRNA.

organelle　A membrane-bounded structure, occurring in eukaryote cells, that has a specialized function. Examples are the nucleus, Golgi complex, and endoplasmic reticulum.

osmosis　The movement of solvent across a semipermeable membrane that separates a solution with a high concentration of solutes from one with a low concentration of solutes. The membrane must be permeable to the solvent but not to the solutes. In the context of cellular osmosis, the solvent is always water, the solutes are ions and molecules, and the membrane is the cell membrane.

osteoblast　Cells that form bones.

ovulation　Rupture of a mature follicle with subsequent release of a mature oocyte from the ovary.

oxidative phosphorylation　Generation of high-energy electrons from food molecules that are used to power the synthesis of ATP from ADP and inorganic phosphate. The electrons are eventually transferred to oxygen, to complete the process; occurs in bacteria and mitochondria.

p53　A tumor suppressor gene that is mutated in about half of all human cancers. The normal function of the *p53* protein is to block passage through the cell cycle when DNA damage is detected.

parthenogenesis　A natural form of animal cloning whereby an individual is produced without the formation of haploid gametes and the fertilization of an egg.

pathogen　An organism that causes disease.

PCR (polymerase chain reaction)　A method for amplifying specific regions of DNA by temperature cycling a reaction mixture containing the template, a heat-stable DNA polymerase, and replication primers.

peptide bond   The chemical bond that links amino acids together to form a protein.

pH   Measures the acidity of a solution as a negative logarithmic function (p) of H^+ concentration (H). Thus, a pH of 2.0 (10^{-2} molar H^+) is acidic, whereas a pH of 8.0 (10^{-8} molar H^+) is basic.

phagocyte   A cell that engulfs other cells or debris by phagocytosis.

phagocytosis   A process whereby cells engulf other cells or organic material by endocytosis. A common practice among protozoans and cells of the vertebrate immune system; from the Greek *phagein,* "to eat."

phenotype   Physical characteristics of a cell or organism.

phosphokinase   An enzyme that adds phosphate to proteins.

phospholipid   The kind of lipid molecule used to construct cell membranes. Composed of a hydrophilic head-group, phosphate, glycerol, and two hydrophobic fatty acid tails.

phosphorylation   A chemical reaction in which a phosphate is covalently bonded to another molecule.

photoreceptor   A molecule or cell that responds to light.

photosynthesis   A biochemical process in which plants, algae, and certain bacteria use energy obtained from sunlight to synthesize macromolecules from CO_2 and H_2O.

phylogeny   The evolutionary history of a group of organisms, usually represented diagrammatically as a phylogenetic tree.

pinocytosis   A form of endocytosis whereby fluid is brought into the cell from the environment.

pixel   One element in a data array that represents an image or photograph.

placebo   An inactive substance that looks the same and is administered in the same way as a drug in a clinical trial.

plasmid   A minichromosome, often carrying antibiotic-resistant genes, that occurs naturally among prokaryotes; used extensively as a DNA cloning vector.

platelet   A cell fragment derived from megakaryocytes and lacking a nucleus that is present in the bloodstream and is involved in blood coagulation.

ploidy   The total number of chromosomes (n) that a cell has. Ploidy is also measured as the amount of DNA (C) in a given cell, relative to a haploid nucleus of the same organism. Most organisms are diploid, having two sets of chromosomes, one from each parent, but there is great variation among plants and animals. The silk gland of the moth *Bombyx mori,* for example, has cells that are extremely polyploid, reaching values of 100,000C, flowers are often highly polyploid, and vertebrate hepatocytes may be 16C.

pluripotency   The property by which an undifferentiated animal cell can give rise to most of the body's cell types.

poikilotherm   An animal incapable of regulating its body temperature independent of the external environment. It is for this reason that such animals are restricted to warm tropical climates.

point mutation   A change in DNA, particularly in a region containing a gene, that alters a single nucleotide.

polarization   A term used to describe the reestablishment of a sodium ion gradient across the membrane of a neuron. Polarization followed by depolarization is the fundamental mechanism by which neurons communicate with one another.

polyacrylamide   A tough polymer gel that is used to fractionate DNA and protein samples.

polyploid   Possessing more than two sets of homologous chromosomes.

polyploidization   DNA replication in the absence of cell division; provides many copies of particular genes and thus occurs in cells that highly active metabolically (see ploidy).

portal system   A system of liver vessels that carries liver enzymes directly to the digestive tract.

post-mitotic   Refers to a cell that has lost the ability to divide.

probe   Usually a fragment of a cloned DNA molecule that is labeled with a radioisotope or fluorescent dye, and used to detect specific DNA or RNA molecules on southern or northern blots.

progenitor cell   A cell that has developed from a stem cell but can still give rise to a limited variety of cell types.

proliferation   A process whereby cells grow and divide.

promoter   A DNA sequence to which RNA polymerase binds to initiate gene transcription.

prophase   The first stage of mitosis; the chromosomes are duplicated and are beginning to condense but are attached to the spindle.

protein   A major constituent of cells and organisms. Proteins, made by linking amino acids together, are used for structural purposes and regulate many biochemical reactions in their alternative role as enzymes. Proteins range in size from just a few amino acids to more than 200.

protein glycosylation   The addition of sugar molecules to a protein.

proto-oncogene   A normal gene that can be converted to a cancer-causing gene (oncogene) by a point mutation or through inappropriate expression.

protozoa   Free-living, single-cell eukaryotes that feed on bacteria and other microorganisms. Common examples are *Paramecium* and *Amoeba*. Parasitic forms inhabit the digestive and urogenital tract of many animals, including humans.

P-site   The binding site on the ribosome for the growing protein (or peptide) chain.

purine   A nitrogen-containing compound that is found in RNA and DNA. Two examples are adenine and guanine.

pyrimidine   A nitrogen-containing compound found in RNA and DNA. Examples are cytosine, thymine, and uracil (RNA only).

radioactive isotope   An atom with an unstable nucleus that emits radiation as it decays.

randomized clinical trial   A study in which the participants are assigned by chance to separate groups that compare different treatments; neither the researchers nor the participants can choose which group. Using chance to assign people to groups means that the groups will be similar and that the treatments they receive can be compared objectively. At the time of the trial, it is not known which treatment is best.

random primer labeling   A method for incorporating labeled nucleotides into a short piece of DNA or RNA.

reagent   A chemical solution designed for a specific biochemical or histochemical procedure.

recombinant DNA   A DNA molecule that has been formed by joining two or more fragments from different sources.

refractive index   A measure of the ability of a substance to bend a beam of light expressed in reference to air that has, by definition, a refractive index of 1.0.

regulatory sequence   A DNA sequence to which proteins bind that regulate the assembly of the transcriptional machinery.

replication bubble   Local dissociation of the DNA double helix in preparation for replication. Each bubble contains two replication forks.

replication fork The Y-shape region of a replicating chromosome; associated with replication bubbles.

replication origin (origin of replication, ORI) The location at which DNA replication begins.

respiratory chain (electron transport chain) A collection of iron- and copper-containing proteins, located in the inner mitochondrion membrane, that use the energy of electrons traveling down the chain to synthesize ATP.

restriction enzyme An enzyme that cuts DNA at specific sites.

restriction map The size and number of DNA fragments obtained after digesting with one or more restriction enzymes.

retrovirus A virus that converts its RNA genome to DNA once it has infected a cell.

reverse transcriptase An RNA-dependent DNA polymerase. This enzyme synthesizes DNA by using RNA as a template, the reverse of the usual flow of genetic information from DNA to RNA.

ribosomal RNA (rRNA) RNA that is part of the ribosome and serves both a structural and functional role, possibly by catalyzing some of the steps involved in protein synthesis.

ribosome A complex of protein and RNA that catalyzes the synthesis of proteins.

rough endoplasmic reticulum (rough ER) Endoplasmic reticulum that has ribosomes bound to its outer surface.

Saccharomyces Genus of budding yeast that are frequently used in the study of eukaryote cell biology.

sarcoma Cancer of connective tissue.

Schwann cell Glia cell that produces myelin in the peripheral nervous system.

screening Checking for disease when there are no symptoms.

senescence Physical and biochemical changes that occur in cells and organisms with age; from the Latin word *senex,* meaning "old man" or "old age."

signal transduction A process by which a signal is relayed to the interior of a cell where it elicits a response at the cytoplasmic or nuclear level.

smooth muscle cell Muscles lining the intestinal tract and arteries; lack the striations typical of cardiac and skeletal muscle, giving a smooth appearance when viewed under a microscope.

somatic cell   Any cell in a plant or animal except those that produce gametes (germ cells or germ cell precursors).

somatic cell nuclear transfer   Animal cloning technique whereby a somatic cell nucleus is transferred to an enucleated oocyte. Synonymous with cell nuclear transfer or replacement.

southern transfer   The transfer of DNA fragments from an agarose gel to a piece of nylon filter paper. Specific fragments are identified by hybridizing the filter to a labeled probe; invented by the Scottish scientist E. M. Southern, in 1975; also known as DNA blotting.

stem cell   Pluripotent progenitor cell found in embryos and various parts of the body that can differentiate into a wide variety of cell types.

steroid   A hydrophobic molecule with a characteristic four-ringed structure. Sex hormones, such as estrogen and testosterone, are steroids.

structural gene   A gene that codes for a protein or an RNA; distinguished from regions of the DNA that are involved in regulating gene expression but are noncoding.

synapse   A neural communication junction between an axon and a dendrite. Signal transmission occurs when neurotransmitters, released into the junction by the axon of one neuron, stimulate receptors on the dendrite of a second neuron.

syncytium   A large multinucleated cell. Skeletal muscle cells are syncytiums produced by the fusion of many myoblasts.

syngeneic transplants   A patient receives tissue or an organ from an identical twin.

tamoxifen   A drug that is used to treat breast cancer. Tamoxifen blocks the effects of the hormone estrogen in the body. It belongs to the family of drugs called antiestrogens.

T cell (T lymphocyte)   A white blood cell involved in activating and coordinating the immune response.

telomere   The end of a chromosome; replaced by the enzyme telomerase with each round of cell division to prevent shortening of the chromosomes.

telophase   The final stage of mitosis in which the chromosomes decondense and the nuclear envelope reforms.

template   A single strand of DNA or RNA whose sequence serves as a guide for the synthesis of a complementary, or daughter, strand.

therapeutic cloning   The cloning of a human embryo for the purpose of harvesting the inner cell mass (embryonic stem cells).

topoisomerase   An enzyme that makes reversible cuts in DNA to relieve strain or to undo knots.

totipotency   The property by which an undifferentiated animal cell can give rise to all of the body's cell types. The fertilized egg and blastomeres from an early embryo are the only cells possessing this ability.

transcription   The copying of a DNA sequence into RNA, catalyzed by RNA polymerase.

transcription factor   A general term referring to a wide assortment of proteins needed to initiate or regulate transcription.

transfection   Introduction of a foreign gene into a eukaryote or prokaryote cell.

transfer RNA (tRNA)   A collection of small RNA molecules that transfer an amino acid to a growing polypeptide chain on a ribosome. There is a separate tRNA for amino acid.

transgenic organism   A plant or animal that has been transfected with a foreign gene.

trans Golgi network   The membrane surfaces where glycoproteins and glycolipids exit the Golgi complex in transport vesicles.

translation   A ribosome-catalyzed process whereby the nucleotide sequence of a mRNA is used as a template to direct the synthesis of a protein.

transposable element (transposon)   A segment of DNA that can move from one region of a genome to another.

ultrasound (ultrasonography)   A procedure in which high-energy sound waves (ultrasound) are bounced off internal tissues or organs producing echoes that are used to form a picture of body tissues (a sonogram).

umbilical cord blood stem cells   Stem cells, produced by a human fetus and the placenta, that are found in the blood that passes from the placenta to the fetus.

vector   A virus or plasmid used to carry a DNA fragment into a bacterial cell (for cloning) or into a eukaryote to produce a transgenic organism.

vesicle   A membrane-bounded bubble found in eukaryote cells. Vesicles carry material from the ER to the Golgi and from the Golgi to the cell membrane.

virus   A particle containing an RNA or DNA genome surrounded by a protein coat. Viruses are cellular parasites that cause many diseases.

western blotting   The transfer of protein from a polyacrylamide gel to a piece of nylon filter paper. Specific proteins are detected with labeled antibodies. The name was inspired by the original blotting technique invented by the Scottish scientist E. M. Southern in 1975; also known as protein blotting.

xenogeneic transplants (xenograft)   A patient receives tissue or an organ from an animal of a different species.

yeast   Common term for unicellular eukaryotes that are used to brew beer and make bread. *Saccharomyces cerevisiae* (baker's yeast) are also widely used in studies on cell biology.

zygote   A diploid cell produced by the fusion of a sperm and egg.

 **Further Resources**

BOOKS

Alberts, Bruce, Dennis Bray, Karen Hopkins, and Alexander Johnson. *Essential Cell Biology.* 2d ed. New York: Garland, 2003. A basic introduction to cellular structure and function that is suitable for high school students.

Alberts, Bruce, Alexander Johnson, Julian Lewis, Martin Raff, Keith Roberts, and Peter Walter. *Molecular Biology of the Cell.* 5th ed. New York: Garland, 2008. Advanced coverage of cell biology that is suitable for senior high school students and undergraduates.

Carbone, Larry. *What Animals Want: Expertise and Advocacy in Laboratory Animal Welfare Policy.* New York: Oxford University Press, 2004. A much-needed overview of the plight of animals used for research.

Ganong, William. *Review of Medical Physiology.* 22d ed. New York: McGraw-Hill, 2005. A well-written overview of human physiology, beginning with basic properties of cells and tissues.

Krause, W. J. *Krause's Essential Human Histology for Medical Students.* Boca Raton, Fla.: Universal Publishers, 2005. This book goes well with histology videos provided free on Google video.

Panno, Joseph. *Aging: Modern Theories and Therapies.* Rev. ed. New York: Facts On File, 2010. Explains why and how people age, and how stem cells may be used to reverse or modify the process.

————. *Cancer: The Role of Genes, Lifestyle, and Environment.* Rev. ed. New York: Facts On File, 2010. The basic nature of cancer written for the general public and young students.

————. *The Cell: Exploring Nature's First Life-form.* Rev. ed. New York: Facts On File, 2010. Everything you need to know about the cell without having to read a 1,000-page textbook.

————. *Gene Therapy: Treatments and Cures for Genetic Diseases.* Rev. ed. New York: Facts On File, 2010. Discusses not only the great potential of this therapy but also its dangers and its many failures.

————. *Stem Cell Research: Medical Applications and Ethical Controversies.* Rev. ed. New York: Facts On File, 2010. All about a special type of cell, the stem cell, and its use in medical therapies.

Renneberg, Reinhard, and Arnold Demain. *Biotechnology for Beginners.* Academic Press, 2007. An interesting book that approaches the subject from an historical perspective.

Wells, H. G. *The Island of Dr. Moreau.* Available online. URL: http://www.online-literature.com/wellshg/doctormoreau/. Accessed December 18, 2008. The full text of this book has been posted on the Internet by the Literature Network.

Wilmut, Ian, Keith Campbell, and Colin Tudge. *The Second Creation.* New York: Farrar, Straus & Giroux, 2000. Wilmut and some of his team discuss their work leading up to the cloning of Dolly.

JOURNALS AND MAGAZINES

Chung, Young, et al. "Reprogramming of Human Somatic Cells Using Human and Animal Oocytes" *Cloning and Stem Cells* 11 (2009): 1–11. This work, headed by Robert Lanza, shows that hybrid embryos fail to develop normally.

Church, George. "Genomes for All." *Scientific American* 294 (January 2006): 46–54. This article discusses fast and cheap DNA sequencers that could make it possible for everyone to have their genome sequenced, giving new meaning to personalized medicine.

Cibeli, Jose. "Is Therapeutic Cloning Dead?" *Science* 318 (December 21, 2007): 1,879–1,880. The author of this article argues that since the creation of iPS cells, therapeutic cloning is no longer needed.

Costello, Joseph. "Tips for Priming Potency." *Nature* 454 (July 3, 2008): 45–46. A news article regarding the problems scientists encounter when producing iPS cells. This article serves as an introduction to a research article in the same issue (see Mikkelsen et al.).

Dimos, John et al. "Induced Pluripotent Stem Cells Generated from Patients with ALS Can Be Differentiated into Motor Neurons." *Sciencexpress* (July 31, 2008): 1–4. Kevin Eggan's team succeed in producing an iPS-based therapy for a neurological disorder.

Kaji, Keisuke et al. "Virus-free Induction of Pluripotency and Subsequent Excision of Reprogramming Factors" *Nature* (March 1, 2009): 1–5. Published online. A new method to produce safe iPS cells.

Moreno-Manzano, V. et al. "Activated Spinal Cord Ependymal Stem Cells Rescue Neurological Function." *Stem Cells* 27 (2009): 733–743. A Spanish team, headed by Mirodrag Stojkovic, has produced an effective method to treat spinal cord injury with AS cells.

Surani, Azim, and Anne McLaren. "A New Route to Rejuvenation." *Nature* 443 (September 21, 2006): 284–285. A news article that discusses the potential of iPS cells.

Takahashi, Kazutoshi, and Shinya Yamanaka. "Induction of Pluripotent Stem Cells from Mouse Embryonic and Adult Fibroblast Cultures by Defined Factors." *Cell* 126 (August 25, 2006): 663–676. The first report to describe the production of iPS cells.

Takahashi, Kazutoshi, et al. "Induction of Pluripotent Stem Cells from Adult Human Fibroblasts by Defined Factors." *Cell* 131 (November 30, 2007): 861–872. Yamanaka's team extend their work by producing iPS cells from human fibroblasts.

Wadman, Meredith. "Stem Cells Ready for Prime Time." *Nature* 457 (January 29, 2009): 516. FDA approves the first clinical trial involving embryonic stem cells.

Watson, James, and Francis Crick. "A Structure for Deoxyribose Nucleic Acid." *Nature* 171 (April 25, 1953): 737–738. Watson and Crick's classic paper describing the structure of DNA. This article is also available on *Nature*'s Web site as a free download.

Wernig, Marius et al. "In Vitro Reprogramming of Fibroblasts into a Pluripotent ES-cell-like State." *Nature* 448 (July 19, 2007): 318–325. Confirmation that iPS cells are similar to ES cells at the gene level.

———. "Neurons Derived from Reprogrammed Fibroblasts Functionally Integrate into the Fetal Brain and Improve Symptoms of Rats with Parkinson's Disease." *PNAS* 105 (April 7, 2008): 5,856–5,861. The first attempt to use iPS cells for a medical therapy.

Wilmut, Ian et al. "Viable Offspring Derived from Fetal and Adult Mammalian Cells." Nature 385 (February 27, 1997): 810–813. Ian Wilmut's now classic paper describing the cloning of Dolly.

Zhou, Qiao et al. "In Vivo Reprogramming of Adult Pancreatic Exocrine Cells to β-cells." *Nature* 455 (October 2, 2008): 627–632. Sidestepping the use of stem cells, these researchers converted one type of pancreatic cell into another (the β-cells).

ARTICLES ON THE INTERNET

Associated Press. "Mule in Idaho Is First Member of Horse Family to Be Cloned." May 29, 2003. Available online. URL: http://www.nytimes.com/2003/05/29/science/29WIRE-MULE.html.

Accessed April 10, 2009. Some background information on Idaho Gem, the first cloned mule.

McKinley, Jesse. "A California Ballot Measure Offers Rights for Farm Animals." *New York Times*. Available online. URL: http://www.nytimes.com/2008/10/24/us/24egg.html?scp=2&s q=california%20proposition%202&st=cse. Accessed April 10, 2009. This article discusses California proposition 2, and is accompanied by a photograph of an egg-processing plant in Atwater, California, that captures the astonishing scale of such operations.

Morales, Lymari. "Majority of Americans Likely Support Stem Cell Decision." *Gallup*. Available online. URL: http://www. gallup.com/poll/116485/Majority-Americans-Likely-Support-Stem-Cell-Decision.aspx. Accessed March 10, 2009. A recent Gallup poll has shown that a majority of Americans favor easing restrictions on embryonic stem-cell research.

National Institutes of Health. "Regenerative Medicine 2006." Available online. URL: http://stemcells.nih.gov/info/scireport/ 2006report.htm. Accessed January 1, 2009. A 62-page pamphlet, written for the general public, describing stem cell research and therapies that may be possible in the future.

Noyes, Dan. "New Ammunition for Prop. 2 Supporters." Available online. URL: http://abclocal.go.com/kgo/story?section=news/ iteam&id=6447851. Accessed April 10, 2009. An ABC video report describing an undercover investigation of a southern California egg ranch.

Pollack, Andrew. "F.D.A. Approves Drug From Gene-Altered Goats." *New York Times*. Available online. URL: http://www. nytimes.com/2009/02/07/business/07goatdrug.html?hp. Accessed April 10, 2009. The drug that was approved is called antithrombin, produced by GTC Biotherapeutics. This is the first time a transgenic drug has been approved for medical use in the United States.

Wall Street Journal. "Wait-Listed to Death." Available online. URL: http://online.wsj.com/article/SB122948107890913051.html. Accessed April 7, 2009. This editorial discusses the controversial issue of allowing incentives for organ donation.

Whitehouse.gov. "The Briefing Room." Available online. URL: http://www.whitehouse.gov/the_press_office/Removing-Barriers-to-Responsible-Scientific-Research-Involving-Human-Stem-Cells/ Accessed April 10, 2009. The text of President Barack Obama's executive order that lifted some restrictions on embryonic stem cell research.

WEB SITES

Abiomed. Available online. URL: http://www.abiomed.com/index.cfm. Accessed April 7, 2009. This company specializes in the production of an artificial heart, known as the AbioCor.

Albumin.org. "Human Serum Albumin." Available online. URL: http://www.albumin.org. Accessed April 7, 2009. This site contains general information about HSA, including an updated list of known albumin mutations.

Centers for Disease Control and Prevention. Available online. URL: http://www.cdc.gov/art/. Accessed March 10, 2009. A U.S. medical site that contains a great deal of information about diseases that are common in North America.

Chimpanzee Sanctuary Northwest. Available online. URL: http://www.chimpsanctuarynw.org/ Accessed April 7, 2009. This sanctuary is dedicated to the goal of giving former research and entertainment chimpanzees a decent place to live.

Department of Energy Human Genome Project. Available online. URL: http://genomics.energy.gov. Accessed April 7, 2009. Covers every aspect of the Human Genome Project with extensive color illustrations.

Genetic Science Learning Center at the Eccles Institute of Human Genetics, University of Utah. Available online. URL: http://

learn.genetics.utah.edu/. Accessed April 7, 2009. An excellent resource for beginning students, this site contains information and illustrations covering basic cell biology, animal cloning, gene therapy, and stem cells.

Geron Corporation. Available online. URL: http://www.geron. com/grnopc1clearance/. Accessed March 10, 2009. The corporation has posted documents describing its clinical trial to treat spinal cord injury with ES cell-derived oligodendrocytes.

Google Video. Available online. URL: http://video.google.com/ videosearch?q=histology+tissue&emb=0&aq =3&oq=histology#. Accessed April 10, 2009. This site contains many videos covering human histology and cell biology.

GTC Biotherapeutics. Available online. URL: http://www.trans genics.com/. Accessed April 7, 2009. This company, profiled in chapter 9, specializes in the production of transgenic drugs.

Hematech, Inc. Available online. URL: http://www.hematech. com/. Accessed April 7, 2009. The company's Web site provides detailed information about their transgenic animals, products, and future goals.

Holstein Canada. "The Holstein Breed." Available online. URL: http://www.holstein.ca/English/Breed/index.asp. Accessed April 7, 2009. Information about the Holstein cow, animal health, and industry statistics.

Human Fertilization and Embryology Authority. Available online. URL: http://www.hfea.gov.uk/. Accessed March 9, 2009. The British government agency that regulates IVF clinics and all research involving human embryos.

Institute of Molecular Biotechnology, Jena, Germany. Available online. URL: http://www.imb-jena.de/IMAGE.html. Accessed April 7, 2009. This site has an image library of biological macromolecules.

International Society for Heart & Lung Transplantation. Available online. http://www.ishlt.org/registries/quarterlyDataReport.asp.

Accessed April 7, 2009. An American Web site, headquartered in Addison, Texas, that provides extensive organ transplantation statistics.

National Center for Biotechnology Information (NCBI). Available online. URL: http://www.ncbi.nlm.nih.gov. Accessed April 7, 2009. This site, established by the National Institutes of Health, is an excellent resource for anyone interested in biology. The NCBI provides access to GenBank (DNA sequences), literature databases (Medline and others), molecular databases, and topics dealing with genomic biology. With the literature database, for example, anyone can access Medline's 11,000,000 biomedical journal citations to research biomedical questions. Many of these links provide free access to full-length research papers.

National Health Museum Resource Center. Washington, D.C. Available online. URL: www.accessexcellence.org/RC/. Accessed April 7, 2009. Covers many areas of biological research, supplemented with extensive graphics and animations.

National Human Genome Research Institute. Available online. URL: http://www.genome.gov/. Accessed April 7, 2009. The institute supports genetic and genomic research, including the ethical, legal, and social implications of genetics research.

National Institutes of Health. Available online. URL: http://www.nih.gov. Accessed April 7, 2009. The NIH posts information on their Web site that covers a broad range of topics, including general health information, stem cell biology, aging, cancer research, and much more.

Nature Publishing Group. Available online. URL: http://www.nature.com/nature/supplements/collections/humangenome/commentaries/ Accessed April 7, 2009. The journal *Nature* has provided a comprehensive guide to the human genome. This site provides links to the definitive historical record for the sequences and analyses of human chromosomes, All papers, which are free for downloading, are based on the final draft produced by the Human Genome Project.

Organ Procurement and Transplantation Network (OPTN). Available online. URL: http://www.optn.org/AR2007/default.htm. Accessed April 7, 2009. Complete organ transplant statistics provided by the U.S. Organ Procurement and Transplantation Network and the Scientific Registry of Transplant Recipients.

Roslin Institute. Available online. URL: http://www.roslin.ed.ac. uk/. Accessed April 7, 2009. The place where Dolly was born is still an important center for the study of animal genetics, biotechnology, and biomedicine.

Science Museum, London. "Dolly the Sheep, 1996–2003." Available online. URL: http://www.sciencemuseum.org.uk/antenna/dolly/index.asp. Accessed April 10, 2009. All about Dolly and the science that led to her birth.

University of Louisville Health Sciences Center."The Implantable Artificial Heart Project." Available online. URL: http://www.heartpioneers.com. Accessed April 10, 2009. Discusses artificial hearts and the patients who have received them.

U.S. Food and Drug Administration. Available online. URL: http://www.fda.gov. Accessed April 7, 2009. Provides extensive coverage of general health issues and regulations.

Index

Note: *Italic* page numbers indicate illustrations.

212